Beloved

Sky View, the Ranch of Refuge

Hannah Swayze

Beloved: Sky View, the Ranch of Refuge
by Hannah Swayze © 2016 by Hannah Swayze

Print ISBN: 978-0-9975319-0-9
eBook ISBN: 978-0-9975319-1-6

Cover and Interior Design: Fusion Creative Works, fusioncw.com

For more information about Sky View Horse Ranch,
contact skyviewhorseranch@gmail.com

First Printing
Printed in the United States of America

"This I recall to my mind,
Therefore I have *hope*.

Through the Lord's *mercies* we are not consumed,
Because His compassions fail not.
They are new every *morning*;

Great is Your *faithfulness*.
'The Lord is my portion,' says my soul,
'Therefore I *hope* in Him!'"

Lamentations 3:21-24 (NKJV)

I would like to dedicate this book

to the heroes of my heart.

My Jesus,

my Daddy,

and the man he will one day entrust my heart to.

I love that you call me *beloved*.

Contents

Foreword

Hannah caught her father's passions early in life: a love for God, a love for people, and a love for horses. Every ride through green pastures to the blackberry patch or into the lakes and mountains of Oregon's wilderness brought a longing to share the horse experience with young people.

As a family we wrestled with how much time we should spend with horses, when there are so many needs among people. We wanted to please our Lord in all ways and the time we spent with our horses seemed somewhat selfish.

Then we toured Crystal Peaks Youth Ranch in Bend, Oregon and discovered that they were living our dream. They were using horses to reach not just a few, but thousands of kids from every situation and walk of life. We were hooked—and Crystal Peaks did everything they could to help us get started. That relationship continues today.

What followed has been an incredible display of God's mighty hand of blessing, His clear direction, and His generous provision.

Our rugged pack horses bred for strength, boldness, tenacity and hard work, now line up at the fence to be hugged, kissed, brushed, adored, washed, fussed over, cried on, confessed to, and ridden by students who are loved by God through these majestic creatures.

Hannah and our staff, along with an army of volunteers, are impacting lives with the love of God, the love of people and the love of horses!

We very much enjoy giving tours of Sky View Horse Ranch and you are invited to come. We can show you the buildings, the trees, the round pens, the arenas, and the horses. You can see kids riding and laughing and families coming and going. What you will not see is the deep need, the hidden pain, the shame and the all-encompassing sense of loss that eat away at the joy of so many children (and parents). They come because they want to be with a horse, and they thrive and heal because of unconditional love and hope. What Hannah has written in these pages allows you to see past the facilities and the program and to look deep into the intentional ministry of the ranch and into the very heart of a loving God.

Blessings on you.

Larry Swayze

Larry Swayze, Founder/Director Sky View Horse Ranch
Hannah's Daddy

Introduction

I looked into the darkest, most pain-filled eyes I had ever met at Sky View. Our ranch had been open for a few short weeks and I had received a call from a foster mom who wanted to bring her girls up to ride the horses. When they stepped out of the car, I could see that Tracy bore the heaviness of a girl who had seen too many horrific things in her short life. Her mom explained to us that this was her last stop—her last chance at a regular home life. If she ran away from their house, she would be committed into the foster system's version of prison. She was hardly old enough to be a teenager, much less in jail.

Over the course of an hour and a half as we talked and worked with the horses, the gravity of the situation became more apparent. Tracy had been adopted years before, and throughout the short time of living with her new family, she was repeatedly abused by her adoptive dad. She had been told over and over that it was all she was made for. So she had been taken from her new family and placed in the safety of foster homes, from which she repeatedly ran, again and again. That day at the ranch was the last that I ever saw of Tracy. I have no idea what happened to her.

When we opened Sky View Horse Ranch with the goal of working with kids—whether at risk, struggling in school, missing a parent, with physical disabilities, or simply needing love—I had no idea of all that we were stepping into. I wept on the drive home, the day I met Tracy. I had begun to realize the magnitude of the trail we were embarking on, into the lives of children ravaged by the enemy of their souls. Despite the struggles and the pain we have encountered, we have pushed on through the years because we can offer what they need: hope, love, redemption, and a Savior. And they come because they simply want to ride a horse.

Years later, I sit in the Sky View tack room. My desk is cluttered with the projects of the days and weeks. Saddles surround me and the faces of my students smile through the glass of framed pictures. As I sip my tea, I look out the window; through it I see an arena. A gate opens to a field, and another opens to the parking lot. Three bay horses graze outside another window. As I sit here, the question arises: how do I convey all that Sky View encompasses, through simple words on a page? Words that could never do justice to the fulfillment of a dream that Sky View has become.

The arena is really just a simple enclosure. A place where a horse can be worked on precision moves and training in a contained area. But when I look at it, what I see is the many hours I have walked around it, shoulder to shoulder with a horse, listening to a child pour out his or her heart. I hear the laughter of kids being nuzzled by horses, the delighted shriek of a girl cantering—flying—for the first time. I see the hurt and feel the sobs of a girl's tears running through a horse's mane as she cries out the pain of a broken past and the longing for a better future. I see more than an arena; I see the heartbeat of Sky View Horse Ranch.

I see the children whose lives we have had the opportunity to touch—lives that have been changed. I see the shy smile of a girl who has just been escorted into the presence of the Most High God, and who stands washed in His blood, with the sins of the past life gone and the new hope of eternal life. I see the boy who struggles with autism, clinging to our horse Satin— much to her chagrin—because he needs a loving hug. I hear kids asking questions from, "Have you ever tried to teach one of your horses to moon walk with its back feet?" to "What's the difference between Christianity and Catholicism?" I see little girls climbing out of the car, calling the names of volunteers, hardly able to contain their excitement as they look forward to the adventures of the day. I envision horses leaning in on the kids who need a hug, and Stripe's ever-present searching for candy canes. It is tears, laughter, prayer, and brokenness all wrapped up in the beautiful love of God. It is where I have the honor of working.

I want to welcome you to Sky View Horse Ranch. If you were here in person, your car tires would have crunched up our gravel driveway as you drove by horses grazing in the trees on either side of you. You would have seen an old-looking western building as you pulled in and an arena would meet you as you pulled into the parking lot. I would step out of the tack room and greet you as you were also met with the smell of fresh woods and horses. My name is Hannah Swayze and I have been working here at Sky View since it opened in 2012. I would hope as we met that you would come here and find far more than a simple place where kids can ride horses. Then I would begin to tell you our dream, the reason we opened Sky View Horse Ranch and the way we have seen God work through it. But it would all still be just a vision until I began to introduce you into the lives of the kids we love and teach. I would begin to tell you their stories. Tears would threaten my voice and eyes as I did my best to convey to you all that the ranch is in my life and in the lives of so many others—a refuge, a safe place. A ranch where dreams have been fulfilled over and over again.

Tears blur the words even now as I write about the heart of the ranch and the kids we so deeply love. Welcome to Sky View Horse Ranch.

"Sweet Grass is helping me get over my fears! I can tell when I look them in the eye if they are going to be a good horse!"

—Sky View Student

One

Chocolate and Vanilla

Two girls, as different as their names—Chocolate and Vanilla—called sisters. They probably would have never met had their lives been different, but they were foster girls; strangers to each other, who were thrown into a family unfamiliar with them, their lives, and even their culture. One was blond, fair, and talkative, and the other olive-skinned, dark haired, quiet, and beautiful. One was familiar with the way horses lived, breathed, and moved, the other terrified of them. Two girls who each on the sunny day in question, set foot on Sky View soil to ride a horse.

I had gotten the phone call that had become all too familiar. It was a mother's plea for help: "I have no idea who you are, but someone gave me a flier. What does your ranch do?" I explained how our program operates and she began to describe the lives of her children to me. They were girls who had not been born to her, but through the cruelest of circumstances had become her daughters. As she, a total stranger, was safer than living with their flesh and blood parents . . . and now she was losing their hearts. Her concern was especially for her oldest daughter. I had a lesson slot open and she jumped at the opportunity to bring both her girls up to the ranch.

So they came on the clear warm day their foster mom had surprised them with the opportunity, in part to have a fun adventure and in part to not let the one afraid of horses have time to worry about the situation. They stepped out of their car—Vanilla excited to breathe the scent of horse again and Chocolate timid.

As their new mom filled out release forms for her daughters, I asked questions and found helmets that would fit them both. Then we took a walk to find the horses. Vanilla said she loved black horses and Chocolate told me her dream horse would be white.

As we climbed the hill, I hung back with Chocolate—trying to learn all I could about her. Vanilla surged on ahead in search of a horse. We found the herd at the top of the hill, calmly eating everything in sight. I held back and watched as Vanilla, who had wanted a black horse, walked right past all of them and stood in front of Simon, our only white horse. She chose the outcast. The herd only puts up with him because he always finds them. No matter how many times they sneak away and lose him in the woods, he manages to discover their hiding spot. After he finds them, they sigh a "better luck next time" and put up with his awkward lack of social skills until the opportunity presents itself to lose him again.

As Vanilla stroked Simon's nose, I watched her fall in love with him. His delicate features with soft brown eyes, looking out through a cream-colored forelock, were stroked with love. She looped the rope over his neck. There were no questions asked, no meeting the rest of the herd. She had found her horse.

Chocolate quietly followed me as I introduced her to each horse. After all the introductions, she made her decision. She had chosen Erik. He was well known at Sky View as the California beach boy. His bleached blond mane and body-builder physique lent to the nickname; the rest came from his dynamic personality. However, she chose him because he was the shortest horse. I haltered him and we led the procession down the mountain to the corrals.

Vanilla was chosen to ride first and we headed out to groom Simon. I explained that he is bullied by the other horses, not well loved, and has trouble fitting in. I watched her groom him as I described him to her. As she worked I talked and it soon became evident to me that I was describing her as well as Simon. I had only just met her, but it was clear to see that she had chosen the horse that she could most sympathize and identify with: a horse scorned and rejected by his own kind, an animal that did not fit into his herd. I told her that we needed to prove to him that we loved him and would take care of him. Then I watched as she groomed her kindred spirit with the gentlest of hands.

Simon was saddled and led to the round pen, where the fair-skinned teenager climbed up on his back. As she guided her newfound friend around the pen, her foster mom filled me in on what she knew of her story. Before me rode a girl who was seen as an accident—a mistake her parents had not wanted to make. She was unwanted and had been in and out of foster homes much of her life. Her move to their home had been the result of her mother threatening to kill her. There was no maternal nurturing, only violence and rejection.

I walked back to her—this most beautiful, valuable creation of God, a human life, sitting on a horse that knew all too well the feeling of being rejected. Walking next to her in the sand of the round pen, I heard her whisper a longing of her broken heart, "I used to go fast on my horse . . ." I had no clue what "her horse" had been, but I know that the fulfilling of a dream can sometimes be the simplest of things, an easy form of love. So I did something that never happens here at Sky View. I watched her dismount and her blond hair bounce down the road and into the tack room on her errand.

She returned with the lunge line, a long rope used to work a horse in a circle, and remounted Simon. Then from the center of the round pen, I guided her horse into a canter. I let her go fast on her first visit to Sky View and she got a taste of freedom. As Simon's feet flew for a moment around the arena, all I could hope and pray for was a release; a brief freedom from the brokenness of her life, that the pain would fall and his flying feet would carry it far away from her. She simply rode, holding onto the saddle, with the strength of the horse flowing under her.

As we finished the lesson time, Vanilla commented to her foster mom. "He's blond like me!" The similarity ran far deeper; they could identify on the level of painful of rejection. I agreed with her, but cosmetically he was not quite right. He needed glasses like she had. I took off my sunglasses, squinted in the sun and put them on Simon's face. He wore them tucked in his bridle as she led him down to the hitching post. As she walked with her matching horse, laughter lilted around us.

I found Chocolate sitting quietly in the tack room talking to a volunteer who was working on a craft. I handed her a pair of boots to put on and we walked out together to groom Erik. As we worked we chatted about life, music, and hobbies. As we saddled, their foster mom made it fairly clear to my dad that Chocolate would probably not want to ride. She had had a bad experience on horses when she was younger and was afraid of them. I did not know all of this at the time and we saddled Erik like any routine lesson. I led him up to the small round pen and showed her how to lead him. When he was warmed up and ready to ride, she stepped up on the mounting block and climbed on.

I let her sit there for a moment; there is a lot to take in from the top of a horse. Then when she nodded that she was ready, we gently took a few timid steps around the arena. She clung to the saddle and slowly, ever so slowly, a smile spread across her face, one of the most beautiful smiles Erik had ever carried.

We stopped and I asked her to move around in the saddle. Could she touch his ears? Then she touched her right toe with her left hand. After the other toe was touched, she grabbed hold of the saddle and we walked again. The lesson was simple; the smile was radiant.

When she was done riding, I sent her with one of the volunteers to unsaddle Erik. As they walked down the hill, the simplicity of a girl and a horse, I stepped out of the round pen and sat next to their mom on the sun-warmed rock. "So what do you think?" Her eyes were full as she answered, "I haven't seen her smile like that . . . ever."

In the five months she had lived with them, what she had feared made her smile the biggest on this day. After a moment's pause, I told their mom that I had that time slot open every week if they were interested in coming back. She nodded, "I would be very interested in coming back . . . but, I would need to know what the cost would be." I had the pleasure of informing her that we are a nonprofit organization and their lessons and time at the ranch would be free.

Her eyes filled with tears as she nodded and wiped her eyes, "I don't know what to say . . ."

We sat in silence as she watched her daughters—girls she had so recently met—swing, laugh, and work at unsaddling a horse. The moment felt more like a gift to me as I sat with her, overlooking the ranch. There was nothing that needed to be said.

Two

From Africa to Horseback

The car was quiet as I watched their dark eyes scan the trees and fields beside the road. My sister and I had driven an hour to pick up three people who were refugees from Africa. I had the youngest daughter up front with me and had asked her some questions, but the language barrier was such that easy communication was not possible. She had found the English words to answer some questions, but she seemed to prefer the silence. Her mom and sister sat behind me watching the same scenery race by. It was a beautiful day.

I had met the oldest daughter, Kamia, months before. They had recently arrived in America and Kamia came to a week of Bible Club, a group I am involved with, which was hosted at their apartment complex. She was tall, stunningly beautiful, and had a personality to match. She was shy but warmed up to us by the end of the week and we were fast friends. That was when God began to prick my heart and whisper, "Bring her to ride a horse." I dismissed it as impossible. There was no way to get her on a horse; she lived too far away and had no car, so I continued to dismiss it.

Then their apartment complex was chosen to be one that we continued to visit on a weekly basis throughout the school year. Though I personally was unable to come consistently, every time I saw Kamia, the same pricking of my heart came. After seeing the horse calendar on her wall, I finally asked, "Do you like horses?" The simple question was met with a shy glance and a huge smile. She nodded. "Have you ever ridden a horse?" That was met with a shake of her head. I was all in; I had to let this lovely young woman experience the joy of riding a horse.

The day their family was scheduled to ride finally came. It was clear, sunny, and warm—the perfect day to try something new. My sister and I showed up at their house, and with much chatter in a dialect we did not even know the name of, they excitedly loaded into the van. I peppered them with questions in hopes of learning where in Africa they came from, the name of their language and why they came to America, but soon let quiet reign. The day held so much unknown as we drove the hour back to the ranch.

The car was quiet as we pulled in the driveway of Sky View. After they signed a release form we found them helmets and grabbed a halter. I was excited as we stepped into the pasture where they would meet our horses. I was almost giddy as I looked forward to introducing them to something I am passionate about. As we walked through the gate into the field, there were no horses to be seen. I expected to take a long walk to find them. I called to the "brown herd" as I latched the gate. We turned and began our walk to find them, but they had heard me. Zion started to call and then I heard the thunder. Stripe, Zion, and Faith came crashing through the trees and up the hill. It was glorious.

I turned to watch the three beautiful women behind me. I wanted to see them as they witnessed such a rich, breathtaking experience. I turned just as they began to shriek. Excitement and fear were in their eyes as all three of them screamed and ran to hide behind me. I was the wall of safety that they ran to as the horses came up to greet us. It was all beautifully overwhelming.

They laughed and peeked out from behind me as 2,700 pounds of curious horses came to investigate the peals of delight and fear. The shrieking and noise grew as the horses came closer. Stepping out from behind me, the younger sister explained that she was afraid the horses were going to "punch her with their feet." I assured her that she would not be hurt and they stepped out from behind me. Dark skin met the curious searching of Zion's nose. The youngest daughter instantly picked Zion as her horse for the day; choosing her was easier than meeting another horse.

We still had one more horse to pick. Kamia gracefully followed me up the hill, alongside her mom and sister, to find her horse. She had specifically wanted to ride a white horse. The bigger herd with the white horse was nowhere to be seen in our upper pasture. When the horses are not visible, it usually requires at least a half-mile walk to find them. I prayed and called them. The "big horses," as we call that herd, are used to me using a very specific call when I need them to come. I usually include food in the bargain to keep them coming back. I shouted, "Yip yip yip yoo," to them and waited. No sign of movement. The girls giggled, joined me in the call, and we tried again.

As we turned to leave, I heard Zephyr call back, and thunder clapped again on the mountain as seven horses came at a dead run down off the ridge and through the trees. The shrieks of delighted terror rang again. When the horses came to a snorting halt at the gate, Kamia followed me timidly into the field and picked her horse. Sweet Grass had enough white on her to more than satisfy.

I placed Sweet Grass's rope in Kamia's hand and then stepped back and walked just far enough behind her to let her spend time with Sweet Grass. As they walked down the hill, long dark fingers timidly reached to touch Sweet Grass' white and chestnut spots. Her smile flashed as she watched Sweet Grass' lips sneaking a few bites of grass. As they walked, Kamia measured her steps to match those of her horse and a gentle, quiet happiness enveloped them.

We walked down the hill and stepped into the round pen. I wanted them to feel the horse's movement, unhindered by the saddle. It took some time, but both girls climbed on bare-back. I introduced them to the feel of a horse by leading them around the arena, they both laughed at the struggle of staying balanced without a saddle. Once we were done in the round pen, we saddled the horses and they willingly climbed onto their horses.

After they had both ridden for a long while with laughter, shrieking, and delight, their mom voiced her wish to try it as well. This single mother, who had fled with her daughters from unknown persecution in Africa, was carried by Sweet Grass into laughter. She smiled deeply and warmly as she got off and finished watching her daughters' delight. It was a per-fect day—God's hand was more than evident.

The car ride home that afternoon was quiet. Sometimes words are hard to find even if you are fluent in the language. When we got back to their apartment, my sister and I got out to say goodbye. After I hugged them, I reached for their mom. She met me with one of the warmest, most grateful hugs I have ever gotten. I think there were tears in both our eyes. How simple a task, to love a woman with so much in her past. How easy it is in the leading of God, to show how greatly she and her girls are loved and valued.

Three

Molasses-Colored Love

Her goal was to get all four of Stripe's hooves on the bridge at once—a monumental task. Each week she sets out to accomplish her goal while she walks Stripe around to warm her up. I am usually busy helping her sister get Sweet Grass ready to ride, but I glance into the arena and see Stripe's methodical testing of patience. She has three hooves firmly on the bridge while one lingers, waiting to take the last step. My student clucks to her and asks for one more step. All four hooves should be planted where the girl wants them, but Stripe, with half closed eyes and not a moment's hesitation, picks the last hoof up and before setting it down moves a front hoof off the wooden structure. My student laughs, feigns frustration, and tries again. She has been riding Stripe for almost a year and I think she has gotten all four hooves on the podium at the same time once.

Looking at Stripe, I see a sweet little old Arabian mare who works hard, loves candy canes, and bosses my horse around. But a while ago I took a good look at who she really is. Our 800 pounds of molasses-colored love is a heart holder. She has ensnared the hearts of so many children who have come to the ranch. She wins their affection by being delighted when they come. Laughter is earned by her appreciation of head rubs and hearts are healed on her back as she helps walk away the hurt of the world. God gave us a treasure of priceless worth in a small mare that eats grass at Sky View.

Stripe entered our life in July 2013. I had gone horse shopping with no money in the Sky View fund and prayed I could find a horse. I found several ads for horses that were $500 or cheaper, but all the horses suitable for kids were even farther beyond our price range. I emailed several people just to see if maybe they would want to donate their horse to a good cause. When I was done, I was a bit discouraged about the whole situation and wondered what I was going to do with so few lesson horses for the summer.

Then I got a couple of calls. The first lady was quick to tell me that her horse was not a good horse for kids, so our conversation ended quickly. The next gal called me and as I began my explanation of what we are doing at Sky View, she interrupted me. "So are you guys believers?" I paused and told her that we are very strong Christian believers. What followed was a sweet conversation of two sisters. I was desperately in need of another horse to do what God had called me to do and she had gotten a new job and knew she could not take her horse with her.

We talked for a long time and I agreed to go look at the horse. I was so excited. Stripe sounded like just what we were looking for. She had been used to do lessons for kids and was accustomed to arena work. As the conversation came to a close I asked her, "You're asking $500 for her?"

"No" she said "I'm not asking . . . I'd like to give her to you." Two very common things happened: I cried and God proved His faithfulness.

I picked up one of our volunteers and we went to see Stripe. She greeted me with the horse version of a smile; perked ears and a sparkle in her eyes. I fell in love. As I rode her I knew that God was placing her into my life and I was delighted. My heart broke however as I watched her owner. She had treasured her so deeply and was missing her already.

We pulled into their driveway a few days later to pick up Stripe. With her composure gathered, her owner told me, "On Friday I couldn't really talk, but I wanted to tell you that Stripe was doing things with you that I have only ever had her do with me." I think in that moment, ownership was transferred and Stripe was on staff.

Her owner said her goodbyes and Stripe climbed into our horse trailer: a new phase of life.

A few short hours later, Stripe stood in the Sky View round pen. I was trying to think of a different name for her; it was the only thing I did not like about her. A group of us gathered around her, laid hands on her, and began to pray over her and the ministry that she would be doing at Sky View. God spoke to me while we were praying. He showed me "her" verse. Isaiah 53:5 says, "By His stripes, we are healed." I will never change her name.

Stripe has been a vehicle for God to bring the healing He paid for on the cross into many hearts and lives. On her back, kids have conquered fear, gained confidence in themselves,

"Are you ready for a challenge?"
"Oh yeah, lets burn this candle!"

and giggled while bouncing to her trot. She is leaving a legacy as she bears the name Stripe, a constant reminder of Jesus' gift to us on the cross. God is blessing all that she does, and healing lies in her wake.

A mother of one of my students gave me a gift—a framed picture of Stripe with her chosen verse printed in bold lettering. In the photo, her eyes are closed and she is dozing in the sun during her lesson. Her rainbow-colored reins are drooped around her neck and her ears are flopped. Looking at the picture, you would never guess that you are looking at one of the ranch's strongest lesson horses. She simply looks like a sleepy little old horse, but God uses her life, and by His gift of Stripe, so many are carried to the healing blood of Jesus Christ.

My Kids

You're my laughter and my sunshine
The sparkle in my eye
You're my heartfelt hugs and kisses
The reason that I cry

You're my pressing into Jesus
A tear stained Bible's page
My hand picked, crinkled roses
The sweet in every stage

You're my upturned smiling faces
My giggles of delight
You're the precious heart of Jesus
I love you with all my might

My daisy chain, summer's delight
Pony tail's bouncing bob
You're my ever needing Jesus
You're the why I love my job

You're my notes and cards and pictures
Crunchy apple and stuffed toy
My endless quotes and laughter
Summer days of purest joy

You're my wonder in each moment
Cat's purr and freckled face
My sparkled boots and giggles
Life's high adventure pace

You're the breath and love and snuggle
The fulfillment of a dream
You're the life that pours through Sky View
Like the water in a stream

I love you

— Hannah Swayze

Four

The Gift of Trust

The girl's leery eyes glanced at my face, lowered to Satin's neck and withers, then raised to gaze steadily at her grandma. They looked down again, grappling to find the courage. The task that I had asked of her was too much. Could she touch the white spot between her horse's ears? She glanced back at me, drew a deep breath, and leaned forward as she looked to her grandma one more time. Security and strength were drawn from the one woman in her life who had not betrayed her.

Tentatively, she leaned forward—reaching the tips of her fingers to the white spot between Satin's ears. Then her right hand stretched to touch the toe of her stylish brown slouch cowboy boot, with the name of her favorite TV show scrawled across it in bold Sharpie. Each movement strengthened by a needy glance in the direction of her grandma.

I asked her to attempt several more things that most kids would usually jump at the opportunity to try, but she did not. She struggled through each simple task I asked of her. She would look down, draw a deep breath, then look to her guardian. Confidence was pulled out of the strength standing just outside the round corral.

Alisha had come to us after hearing of our ranch on the radio. As Talitha, one of our faithful volunteers, led her around the round pen, I talked with her grandma. What I heard was another heartbreaking story of a mother's drunken boyfriend stealing the innocence of a little girl. Trust was broken beyond all measure as her mother repeatedly sided with the man who had harmed her. In place of security, Alisha was pushed into a life filled with the horrible memories of abuse, a mother's denial, and heartbreaking abandonment. Grandma had been the tangible safety through the struggles and a rock to which Alisha clung.

The summer sped by as each week, Alisha came to ride the mare she had chosen. Each week she let me take her hand and lead her a little farther out of her comfort zone. Satin's warmth and patience held her other hand as together we led her deeper, from riding bareback to lying back on Satin's rump. Alisha went from clinging in terror to the horn of Satin's saddle to confidently guiding her bareback around the arena.

As the weeks passed, court dates were tossed around and Alisha prepared to face the man who hurt her in order to testify against him in a courtroom. Nightmares and fear overshadowed the whole experience. Through it all, the new safety she had found in the saddle beckoned. She came each week, ready to ride away from the struggles of the past seven days.

Her lesson day dawned bright and clear, and Alisha chose to ride Satin bareback. She found comfort in the closeness of her warmth. After the lesson was over, she lay down on Satin's neck, breathing in the age-old smell of a horse. I let her have some time alone and went to sit by her grandma. We visited by the round pen in the warm sunshine, as Alisha stayed on Satin's back. All too soon, our hour and a half was over and it was time for us to take Satin's bridle off and put her away.

I walked over by Alisha and told her softly that it was time to be done. No response. Satin dozed and I reached up to touch Alisha's knee. My touch stirred her and she jerked awake. Groggy eyes looked back at me and I realized I had interrupted her sweet sleep of total trust. A little girl had found a safe place—free of nightmares—on the back of a horse. Restful sleep, that was so hard to come by, had encompassed her for a short time of freedom.

They found refuge in the confines of Sky View Horse Ranch. A listening ear, love to share, and hugs without end met them as grandmother and student pulled through the gate each week. Then one day, as Talitha walked with Alisha to find Satin, I sat down beside her grandma to talk. Through the course of the conversation, she shared that her granddaughter, who had in a moment of abuse been forced to grow up so quickly, was given the freedom to be a little girl again at the ranch. The change was slow, but each week the freedom lingered a little bit longer as they drove away from the ranch.

As I hugged Alisha goodbye, after the lesson that day, I held her and whispered, "I love you." With a sigh, my sweet little caterpillar, cocooned in fear from the dangers of this world, took yet another step in the process of becoming the beautiful butterfly God has meant for her to be. She sighed, paused, then whispered back, "I love you too." The walls of fear continued to crumble under the freedom of trust.

• • • •

Alisha jumped out of their car, water bottle in hand and a smile on her face. I hugged her and her grandma hello, then smiled as the light happy chatter flooded out the door; she and one of our volunteers searched for her helmet size.

I sat in the shade—a rare pleasure—with her grandma. Alisha and her new friend took the long hike to go find Satin. As we sat together, Grandma spilled her heart; the love for her granddaughter, the weight of all that the week entailed and the struggles faced since the last lesson.

Then the happy chatter returned. Triumphant Alisha, atop a captured Satin, visited from her place of safety. She climbed off, retrieved the brushes, and brushed Satin's black and white spots to shine in contrast. A saddle followed the brushing and soon a rider. Her brown slouch cowboy boots tapped against the silky sides of her beloved horse and they were off once more on their hour of adventure and freedom from the world.

When both horse and rider were warmed up and ready, I took them on their first ever "trail ride." It consisted of her following close at my heels as I walked through the woods of our pasture. Alisha chatted as she kept Satin's nose as close to my pockets as she could.

We wandered through the green beauty and I asked her questions. It was the last lesson of the summer and I was inquiring to see what God had done for her while atop Satin. "What's the biggest thing you have learned this summer?" The little girl on the strong back of our biggest horse paused. She had had everything taken—her innocence, her mother's love and devotion, her childhood, and trust—and she responded with a whisper. Some of the greatest words ever spoken to me at the ranch still stick with me today. My back was turned as the quiet words caught up to my ears and overwhelmed my heart. Grief and joy flooded me as my little girl, broken and torn by the world, whispered, "I've learned to trust."

Five

The Best Day

I led Sweet Grass at a trot around the arena. She followed me begrudgingly, as a novice rider bounced around on her back. I looked back at Jacob and his stiff, white-knuckled grip on the saddle horn. He had never trotted before so as I slowed her back to a walk, I asked him, "What do you think?" A quiet, young boy responded with a nod and an "I like it." I pursued more conversation and asked him why. Without skipping a beat, Jacob threw both arms in the air and almost yelled, "'Cause I want to be a champion!"

I chuckled and continued on with the lesson without giving it much more thought. He came week by week and, sooner than expected, the summer was coming to a close. Our staff had decided that we wanted to award a ribbon to each student, highlighting something that they had done well.

Someone had gifted us with horse show ribbons, so we wanted to share them with our kids.

My little champion stepped out of his car on one of the last days of lessons, ready to ride. His autism sometimes made it hard for him to stay focused through a lesson. In order to keep him involved, we played games requiring a lot of attention and concentration. We hid marbles under caution cones and he would have to find them while riding his horse. He would sit on his horse and throw marbles into a ring in the sand. And he also worked on teamwork skills by tossing marbles from horseback into a cone that Grant, our volunteer, faithfully held for him to aim at.

Each day our lesson revolved around focus and stick-to-it-iveness. He worked hard—we worked hard—and lessons had gone well. Then the final day came. As Grant and I brought the lesson to a close, I climbed the tack room ladder to rummage through the ribbon box. Along with the colorful first- through sixth-place ribbons, there were a few champion awards. The two-tone colors and bold "Champion" written in gold letters down the front caught my eye. This was Jacob's ribbon.

I raced back down the stairs, scrawled "Focus" in the lines on the back of the ribbon, and met Jacob at the door with Grant. With all the pomp and flair I could muster, I called the attention of all who were at the ranch. Siblings gathered around and his mom paused her conversation. I announced that Jacob had won a ribbon. I asked him if he remembered wanting to be a champion. He nodded.

I pulled the ribbon from behind my back and announced, "Jacob, you have won the 'Champion of Focus' award!" Everyone clapped and cheered. Blue eyes sparkled at the world as he took his ribbon and with a flourish placed a hand on his stomach to bow. Then, not wanting to make the requested speech, he stepped from the limelight into the tack room.

The ribbon hung on his shirt for the rest of the day as his sisters rode. While I was giving a lesson, Grant had gone over to the horse toy box. He was putting hinges on it so the lid was easier to open and the toys would be easier to get to while teaching a lesson. I noticed Jacob leaning on the big wooden box, close to his friend. He was simply spending time with a man he enjoyed. As Grant worked, he heard Jacob, talking almost to himself say, "This has been the best day of my life."

My Treasure

You've asked a simple treasure
That I would give my heart
You've asked of me my lifeblood
That I'll gladly do my part

So I offer up my priceless gift
The love I hold inside
I'll bear it to the world
Though I long so much to hide

For as I face the world
I see its hurt so deep
And for Your precious children
I simply have to weep

So I'll lay my heart wide open
Let the scars run deep and long
And I'll cry while they are hurting
For in my weakness You are strong

I only ask that You uphold me
Remind me You are there
And please don't let it shatter
Or crush beyond repair

For it's all I have to offer
At Your feet I'll let it lie
But I ask You, Daddy hold it
And please don't let it die

"This must be what heaven feels like."

Six

The War Horse

Losing one of our horses is one of the hardest experiences here at Sky View, for they truly are warhorses. Although not the type you see in the pictures, clad in armor and flowing fabric and bearing some knight in a jousting tournament, they are horses who war alongside us in showing kids their value. They make war against the words of an abusive person that drag on the young girls. They help us war against low self-image, showing the children that they, in fact, are lovable.

Our warhorses bear the duty of walking away the heavy tension of visiting a hurtful parent, the painful memories, and carry the hearts of those who ask the simple question: Am I lovable? They bear the weight on their backs of those who are broken, sick, and shattered from the pain of this world as we love on them and introduce them to the saving knowledge and the hope of Jesus. While being ridden, they not only carry hurting hearts and catch falling tears but they cause those working with them to smile, despite the past, the hurt, and the pain.

Such was Sable. Sable could chase away any tear and soothe any struggling heart with the warmth of her hug. She was the horse with contrary ears and a heart big enough to love even the most broken kids—one of the greatest warhorses Sky View has ever seen. I had the pleasure of working alongside her, seeing the delight she managed to bring to world-worn souls. She never failed in her mission. And she will be missed far more than anyone will ever realize.

As I step more and more into the heart of God, I am learning to understand why Jesus wept. As He stood before an open tomb, surrounded by the effects of the curse—Adam's decision to disobey, death, sorrow, grief, and loved ones' loss. He knew the final outcome, yet He wept. The pressing weight of His loved ones' loss brought forth tears. Not hopeless sobbing, but gentle weeping as He watched the pain of those He loved and had come to save. The Creator was one in sorrow with His created.

I felt that weight the day it finally broke and Regan's walls fell. As she rode, we talked and she, with some coaxing, allowed me to see the brokenness of her past. As I wrapped my arms around a girl leaning into the earthy, comforting smell of a horse's neck, I wept. The hurt of what she was crying out mingled my tears with hers, there in the arena.

I was not the one that had been hurt, but my heart was breaking as I watched the pain of a beloved student walking through an old wound. She was opening it to the light, allowing me to help her through the hurt, to re-open the wound and clean out the infection of trying to hide the past. Sobs racked her body as I held her. Stripe stood still—a pillar of strength to lean on and I simply began to pray, leading the way into the presence of the King of Kings.

We had lost Regan's horse Sable in the spring. After discovering that she was limping and unable to find a cut or reason, we had started her on penicillin, an antibiotic for horses. The next day Sable was worse. After a call to our vet, we upped her dose of penicillin and continued to care for her. What followed was a discovery of a puncture wound up on the inside of her thigh. Her leg was swollen and she was sick.

No horse has ever been braver than the horse who will let a human hurt them in order to make them better. I nearly wept as I led a limping, struggling horse to the back of our horse trailer. We needed to get her to the advanced care of the veterinarian's office. The exertion to get in was almost more than she could handle. But with encouragement, strokes of love, and patience, she gathered the strength and climbed in.

Over the course of our lessons, I had gleaned a lot of the past from Regan's mom. There was hurt beyond measure, broken trust, and abuse inflicted by a man she should have been able to trust, her father. Week after week as she rode, I looked for ways to open the doors for healing conversation, but nothing came. So I prayed. I prayed for my hurting little girl and asked God what my role was to be. Then He showed me through Sable.

Regan's drooping horse, Sable, stood in the vet's parking lot. As the vet walked up to her, he shook his head, "I'm going to tell you now that the prognosis is not good." He looked at her gums; despite our efforts, the discoloring of dehydration was evident. He slipped a silver needle into a vein and drew out dark thick blood. Another head shake.

Sable had a rare kind of infection, the type that you would not suspect. We had been able to kill the original infection with the penicillin, but the wound had somehow caused the muscles to create a toxin. Her muscles were poisoning her blood. One of the hardest things I have ever done was lead her into a stall at the vet's clinic, hug her good bye, and walk away. He needed room to flush her system with IVs in hopes of flushing out the infection and we would have only been in the way.

When a horse gets hurt, one of the most deadly wounds it can receive is a puncture wound. It is a wound that looks small on the outside, simply a small incision or scabby-looking cut, but if investigated further, it goes deep. The problem with a puncture is that you never know how deeply the horse is hurt, so the wound can fester, infect and eventually kill if it is not dealt with properly. When you are dealing with a puncture, you have to make sure that it heals from the inside out and does not seal over. As I had been praying for Regan in the previous weeks, this came to mind.

As Regan came to the ranch, week after week, year after year, I had seen the wound heal over, a deep puncture evidenced only by a small 'scab'. On the outside there was so little to see, minor insecurities, but as I walked laps around the arena with her, I learned the depth of her puncture wound.

After much prayer, I walked beside Regan during her lesson. Sable had been her horse and I compared her wound to Regan's life as I walked with her. She had covered the hurt, healed it over and pretended it was not there. I prayed internally as I asked her to share with me the hurt of her past; could she tell me the whole story?

It was like tearing open a painful scab as she verbalized and dug up the festering past. I walked with her through the pain because I was not willing to stand by and let the depth of her wound rob her of life. Her life, forever altered in a decision made by her father was once again changed as she revisited the past. Tears rolled off Stripe's neck as sobs racked her rider's body. Going back to the beginning of the story was where healing had finally begun. She rode for a long time that day. Stripe walked as she wept quiet tears. When I hugged her good bye that day I asked, "Did God speak?" she answered me with a confidant "Not yet, but He's going to."

Sable, the namesake of my dad's first horse, and a treasured friend of many students, died gracefully the morning after we took her to the vet's office. To say that Sky View grieved was an understatement. The vet had given her large amounts of painkillers to ease the hurt and he said she was one of the sweetest horses he had worked with. The loss of a beloved friend to a seemingly small wound was hard to handle. However through the painful loss of our little mare, God had opened the door to healing for an even more beloved student. Sable's life was a life well lived.

Seven

#1 Riding Instructor

Winning a gold medal seems to appeal to lots of us. We all want to do something great and have the world applaud as we stand up for all to see and receive a medal. It is something we seem to want, a longing for something more—the desire to be all that we can, fulfillment, hands applauding our value.

But what do those with a gold medal feel at the end of each day? Are they fulfilled in what they do? Do they feel like they have "arrived" when they stand on the podium and receive their award? As the world's applause sounds in their ears, is it enough? All too soon the clapping ceases, the fans go home, and they are left to their own thoughts of fulfillment.

Years ago, I gave the life I live to God. I was in an accident involving a loss of brakes on my bicycle, a steep hill, and a moving van, after which doctors told me I should not be alive. A few days after the wreck, I lay on the couch in the basement.

Laying there in the dark, I took stock with God. I was alive—a miracle. The doctors said I should have been dead, so I was alive for a purpose: to live, sold out for Him. He saved my life, so my life was His to do with what He wanted. Whenever the world's applause becomes tempting, I usually crawl into a quiet place and take account with God.

By retelling Him that I am sold out to Him, I remind my heart that I am working toward a much higher goal: to fall at the feet of the Creator of life and hear Him whisper, "Well done." How much richer His voice will be than any anthem or precious medal. Nothing on earth can compare to the sweetness that moment will hold. The earth is too temporal.

What is amazing is that God sees fit to give us encouragement in our resolve. That He reminds us that what we do and who we are, is important. My encouragement often comes embodied in blonde hair and freckles, in a girl named Gracie. She comes once a week with a smile that glows. As she presents me with my weekly treasure, she tilts her head with a mischievous grin, and pulls it from behind her back; I release my signature gasp of amazement. Gracie's art decorates my bulletin board, her apple gifts have been my lunch and each card and toy horse is a treasure.

The Sky View staff has dubbed these little treasures from our students "paychecks," because they are of far more value than any monetary compensation. We are rich in treasures, cards, and pictures gifted from the grateful hearts of many kids. On a warm, sunny summer morning, my blond-haired, freckled friend handed me a treasure—a blue board with a black horseshoe painted on it. It completely baffled me. Inside the horseshoe there was important writing, but I was clueless as to deciphering it. The conundrum sat on my desk all week, waiting the return of my little beam of sunshine.

She skipped back into ranch life the next week and, after petting the cows, came to see me. As she grabbed her helmet and halter and ran back outside to wait for me to finish talking to her mom, I asked her mom, "What does this say? I love it, but I can't read it." With a squint, she determined that it said, "#1 Riding Instructor."

What more could a woman ask for than to be the #1 riding instructor in a child's life? I felt like I had received a gold medal in the quiet of the tack room. No anthem played, no clapping resounded . . . just a quiet gift made with love. This gift represented the honor of being important in the life of a child and God quietly reminded me that He sees what I do. The lives we live in service to Him are far greater than anything the world has to offer because when we lie down at night, there is peace in knowing we are serving the Most High God and there is nothing better than that. Besides, what Olympian has a plaque that declares them to be the #1 Riding Instructor?!

After the summer, my little blonde went back to school and life fell into a routine without seeing her. As life moved on, something she had told me frequently ran through my mind. She had never been to any kind of a horse show. My mind, though belonging to a grown woman, is still a little horse crazy. I could not comprehend the fact that she had never been to any kind of horse event. So her mom and I plotted and schemed to take her to the horse races at Portland Meadows. The day finally came and she was out of school for Christmas break. We arranged to meet at the racetrack right before post time.

I climbed out of my car and was headed inside when I heard her yell my name. A little girl who I would have never known, had I not been involved in horses, came running at me full speed. A gust of wind blew her black cowboy hat off her head and sent it skittering across the parking lot as she ran toward me. I caught my wind-blown little girl as she jumped into my arms from a dead run.

As I held her, telling her how much I had missed her, my heart could not have been fuller. I was encompassed in the absolute peace of complete fulfillment. With her arms wrapped around my neck in a bear hug, the thought hit me: true fulfillment and absolute contentment are right in the center of God's will. There was no applause, no cameras flashing, and no medal—just the absolute joy of knowing that God had put me in the life of this little girl because I was willing to be in His service. And there is no greater joy than being in the service of the King.

Eight

Hoofprints

Fall had come, and with it the ever-present mud. I was walking out of the pasture when I saw it imprinted in the mud, the perfect outline of Stripe's delicate little hoof. Her Arabian ancestry is so clearly seen in everything about her from her tiny hooves to her dished face. What stopped me, though, was not the perfectness of her hoofprint, but the fact that there was an even smaller hoofprint placed directly inside of it. Stripe had been followed. A small horse named Nickie trailed her, not only through learning the skills of life, but around the pasture as well.

Nickie's mother was an addict. From the day she was foaled, her life had been spent living in the shadow of her mom's need for a fix. Nickie was an unexpected accident. No one even knew that her mother was pregnant until the morning they looked out in the field and saw her wobbly legs sprawling under her as she tried to nurse. Her mother had nothing to give her, emaciated by her addiction.

She was a wind sucker—a horse that gets a "high" by biting onto wood, pulling back, straining, and gasping in a short breath. The motion somehow releases an endorphin that they can become addicted to. Autumn, Nickie's mother, was the worst case I have ever seen. She was starving herself to death because she was too busy gasping in each new surge of high to eat.

They came to the ranch when Nickie was just a couple months old. Autumn became an object lesson, showing the full depths of where an addiction can lead. She was in absolute bondage because she had allowed herself to be controlled by an endorphin. The cruelty of sin was played out through the destruction of her life.

At the same time, I had a student who was lured by the ever-present call of drugs. She stood simply watching the crazy cycle of addiction played out before her. Eyes that had been glazed with meth watched Autumn. It was evident how her addiction had ravaged her body and affected the lives of those around her, namely her baby. Autumn's actions were speaking louder than I ever could, as she set her teeth on whatever she could, strain, pull back, and gasp for air. Her fix was momentary and she would do it again and again and again.

It quickly became evident that Nickie was suffering from her mom's decisions. She was dropping weight instead of gaining. We began to grain her mother in hope that the protein and goodness of food, would work through her system and nourish the milk for the little one whose life depended on her. Once the grain worked into her system, Autumn gave up on grazing at all as she declined faster and faster. Starvation loomed as we did what we could to keep her alive.

The days wore on as it got closer and closer to the time we could wean Nickie and she could nourish herself. Her mother rarely left the panel on which she wind-sucked. I would watch in sorrow each day when I set her grain down in front of her. She would ravenously shove her nose to the bottom of the bucket, then mid-chew, reach over and bite the panel, gasping in air. After she gasped, she would shove her nose back into the bucket to fill her mouth as full as she could before reaching over for another high. Nickie stood in the shadow of her mom's addiction, slowly drifting further and further away from the one God designed to protect her in search of grass.

The three months a foal needs to be able to nurse wore on slowly. As Nickie drifted further and further away, Autumn deteriorated more and more. Three months to the day came and we weaned Nickie; shortly after, we put Autumn down. It was the most humane thing we could do. Nothing had worked to save her, and she was starving herself to death. Nickie did not even seem to notice; she was simply alone. She hunted food and pushed away any attempt on my part to be friendly. She was alone, unskilled in horse social skills, and fending for herself.

Stripe lived in the same field as Nickie. Stripe walked a path worthy of imitation and she soon took Nickie in under her care. As Nickie adjusted to the freedom of not living in the shadow of her druggie mom, she began to follow Stripe. She grazed, gained weight, and began to learn the attributes of a horse. It was shortly after Stripe's "adoption" that I found Nickie's hoofprint encircled by Stripe's.

I began to think of the footprints and hoofprints that wander through our lives. Stripe was living a life worthy of imitation, and she was followed by a young, hurting, baby. How simple Stripe's job was, to love and care for a lonely orphan horse. How simple our life is, to live worthy of imitation—love and care for those around us, and follow the footprints of Jesus, and then we will make an impact.

Stripe almost daily places impacting hoofprints into the lives of the kids who ride her. By simply doing what she does well, she makes an impact. It causes me to wonder how many lives I am making footprints in. Walking in the footprints of Jesus, do I leave a trail? An "imitate me as I imitate Christ" set of footprints that those who come behind me can walk in?

"I feel like such a cowboy riding through fields of flowers!"

Nine

The Shadow of a Horse

She was dying. Skin stretched over bones that had born the weight and burden of many years; her body showed signs of the many young she had carried, nourished, and raised. Life had been full for Shadow and she was tired. Her teeth were worn by age and she preferred lying comfortably in the soft shavings around the ranch rather than searching for grass.

I pulled into the Sky View parking lot and my heart tore. Some of the many tears spilled at the ranch found their way down my cheek, as I watched a faithful friend living her last few days, stretched out in the sun. I had a student coming for a lesson and I needed the elegant Shadow not to be lying in the flowerbed when she arrived. I went over to where she lay, scratched her gently, and then coaxed her to get up. Shadow climbed to her feet, snorted deeply, checked our old tack room for any grain she could reach to satisfy her sweet tooth, then wandered off in search of some green grass worth chewing.

My student came—a beautiful chattering girl—ready to conquer the world on Stripe's back. Her brother climbed out of the car too, with long brown hair nearly brushing his deep blue eyes. This little ten-year-old boy adored horses. His stuffed bear, "Bear Bear," was with him. While his sister and I brushed and saddled Stripe, I let him brush Shadow. Shadow's eyes were warm and as soft as melted chocolate as he brushed her. She stood, at peace with the world, as he leaned on her, stroked her, and visited with her.

As his sister rode and talked in the round pen, I watched God use a horse once again to minister to His beloved children. Shadow spent the whole 90 minutes on her feet, spending time with her young visitor. He led her around on a quest for the best food, all the while petting, leaning on her, and watching her munch the clumps of grass they found. A boy who normally does not like physical contact dwelt in the warmth and love of an old horse. Shadow, floppy eared and content, followed him around.

When the lesson was over, the family said goodbye to Shadow, climbed into their car, and drove off smiling and waving. Once the car had disappeared over the hill and down the driveway, Shadow wandered back over to her favorite pile of shavings and, with a satisfied moan, lowered herself to the ground. She had earned her rest.

We had to put Shadow down about a week later. My vision blurred and my throat ached as I hugged a friend of ten years for the last time. A sweet horse who had come to our family as an old lady. She carried my dad over many mountains, caught many tears, raced my horse and me through fields of chaff. She took my sister on many adventures on her back, side by side with my horse and me, and pushed with a final love to spend time and show value to a little boy who needed a friend. We buried her next to Sable and Sky View grieved their loss.

Pigpen

She tiptoed toward the pigpen
Drawn by seductive cry
And seeing the mud that beckoned
She thought she'd give it a try

So she gently dipped a toe in
And giggled at the feel
Then she stepped and worked in deeper
Unaware of all it would steal

Her feet were brown and muddy
As she climbed out that night
If she could keep it hidden
Everything would be alright

But then as she was walking by
It called her loud and clear
And she ran and stuck her feet in
Sinking deeper without fear

HANNAH SWAYZE

She laughed and stuck her hands in
It felt so good to be alive
As the muck caressed and whispered
Calling her to dive

But she knew that she'd gone far enough
The mud above her knee
As she snuck home in the darkness
Afraid that one would see

But the morning brought a passion
A hunger to play in the silt
As she muddily got herself ready
She smiled and stuffed her guilt

It greeted her with gladness
As she sank to fill her need
For she'd made her decision
His tender voice she'd finally heed

As he spoke his sensual passion
Fulfilling her desire
He took her hand so softly
And led her deep into the mire

BELOVED

She smiled at the pleasure
As he came so soft, so near
And she simply let him have her
Without a thought of fear

Until she surfaced kicking
Just trying to get air
And she pulled back and looked away
From sin's prying lustful stare

As she fought to pull away
"I must go" was her soft cry
And he laughing leaned into the silt
"I'd like to see you try"

"For girl while we were playing
The walls became too steep to climb
And now all that you're good for
Is to wallow in the grime"

Then he reached and pulled her to him
"Your soul is mine to keep"
Then he dove and drug her with him
In the black consuming deep

And there she was molested
By the pigpen's lustful play
As she broke and was submitted
To his passion's wicked way

After many years she lay there
Consumed by guilt and fear
As he stood above her laughing
She broke beneath his leer

For all the walls were screaming
Her guilt and lack of worth
And she cowered in the lonely
As it daily brought him mirth

Until she cried out sobbing
And fell onto her face
And through the empty screaming
A sweet voice filled its place

It was a gentle whisper
Too soft to barely hear
But it rang into her broken depths
So sweet and strong and clear

BELOVED

And as the pigpen screamed
She chose to hear His voice
As He whispered to her heart
She had to make her choice

And then she fell, repentant
Engulfed in sorrow's wave
"Dear Jesus please forgive me"
Then His scarred hand reached to save

She fell before Him broken
"I'm sorry I stepped in
I'm sorry I let it lure me
Please, forgive my sin"

As she lay before Him
She was washed to the purest white
The sweet voice whispered "You're forgiven
And I love you with all My might"

"Mom, I'm gonna ride over to the cowboy town and get some oatmeal!"

Ten

The Reality of a Dream

Dreams are tricky sometimes. They do not often line up with reality, but then again, sometimes God arranges it so that they do. I had dreamed of working with kids and horses for years. Then one day I looked up and realized I am living my dream. I stand in the midst of the trees that surround Sky View Horse Ranch and I often stop to smile at God's fulfillment of my desires. I get to ride a horse to work. I spend my day outside, inviting children to experience the awe and wonder of riding one of creation's most amazing animals. Then in turn, I get to invite them to meet the Creator of their beautiful horse. I laugh at their comments, cry over their hurts and end each day fulfilled in the living of a dream. I have an amazing job.

God told Joshua, after the Israelites miraculously crossed the Jordan River at flood stage, to have each man pick up a huge rock and stack them in a pile. The pile remained and God told them to do it so that future generations would ask them, "Hey Daddy, what's that big pile of rocks for?" The father could tell the story with the message, "God was faithful."

Sky View does not have a literal pile of stones, at least not for that reason, but we do have a faithful God who has led us to where we are now. He has taken so many dreams and fulfilled, expounded on, and improved them. He has allowed my family and me to open Sky View Horse Ranch. But the story goes back much further than the placing of the sign and the saddling of the first horse.

The first dream that God fulfilled was one of a strong, godly man who wanted to leave an inheritance to his children. Gilbert Borg never had schooling past the eighth grade and worked a regular job all of his life. His life left a heritage of wealth far beyond any monetary value. The first stone of the Sky View vision was laid by my grandpa, a strong Norwegian man, who led his family in a godly way. Because of how he raised my mother, she was willing to go into ministry with my dad.

In the few days before he died, my grandfather was surrounded by the fruit of his life—his entire family. Pastors, missionaries, godly mothers, teachers, craftsmen and husbands, who are all devout followers of Jesus, gathered around him in his final moments. The heritage he was leaving was an entire family in love with the God he had served. He had done his job well. We were all there, gathered in his room and we sang him to the gates of Heaven. The angels took over the singing as the patriarch died. With his passing, he left each of his children the greatest gift: a loving family and love for Jesus.

The second dream that God fulfilled was that of my parents. For many years, my family had tried to purchase more property than our five acres and had looked at many options. Beautiful rolling green meadows, streams, houses, barns, and so many other things attracted us to multiple different places over the years. We wondered how we would be able to afford it. If we sold our five acres, if this, if that, and each time when it seemed like it might work, God closed the door and, heartbroken, we would all fall back into the routine of life. Thinking that we would probably never move off our five acres, my dad would encourage us saying, "Well maybe God has a ranch for us somewhere." I would almost scoff out loud thinking, "How on earth would we ever be able to afford a ranch when we can't even afford a small farm?" I doubted that God could do it. Little did I realize that God works in the realm of impossible.

Among his worldly possessions, my grandpa left a will that gave each of his six children a portion of the land they had grown up on. My mother split a small filbert orchard with her older brother. It was zoned industrial and had to be sold, so our family took the profit from it and, after years of waiting, bought a bare piece of land outside of Molalla, Oregon.

I will never forget the day that I first walked on the land that was our dream. My dad had taken me up to see the place he had found. We stood on the ridge overlooking the valley.

It was an overgrown 80 acres that had simply been left as wild forest, only to be logged now and then. The trees were in different stages of growth and the stumps, blackberries, and scotch broom ran wild. It was nothing like what I had been expecting; I had a different picture in my mind. I remember looking down on it and thinking, "That little bit is 80 acres?" I had not walked the fence line yet to realize how big it truly was. My family had prayed for land and God gave us the gift of land.

Another stone was laid by my parents. My father laid a foundation in our family that prioritized ministry and a love of serving our Jesus. He has served all over the world. Before I was born, God called him to full-time ministry with teens. He worked for Youth for Christ for many years; he has spoken all over India, Mexico, and taught the Bible to school teachers in Estonia right after the Berlin Wall fell. He patterned what it meant to "go into all the world and preach the gospel." My mother helped him lay the foundation by praying and teaching us to walk in a manner worthy of the Lord. She taught us how to live our Christian faith in school, with friends and with the neighbor kids.

Then there was my dream, one that I thought I held alone—then realized that my dad shared it: the dream to work with kids and horses, to mesh two of the passions of my life. I had looked into applying to ministries that were doing just that, but none of them seemed to be the right fit so I had begun to think that, in service to Him, God might ask me to set aside the dream of horses.

Then it happened. Another dream fulfilled. A rock of remembrance placed. In the spring of 2012, God answered my prayer. A group of us had gone to the Warm Springs Indian Reservation to work with the amazing kids there over spring break. Crystal Peaks Youth Ranch is also in that area, so on one of our rest mornings, we drove over there. We saw how little facility they really needed to impact the number of lives they had touched. The dream I had had since I was young, of working with kids and horses, looked closer to reality. In talking to my dad and hearing his heart, we decided to embark on one of the greatest adventures of my life.

We broke ground, cleared vines, moved dirt, and sank some posts. Round corrals were roughed out of the forest. An outdoor arena was laid out and the stumps in it pulled and burned.

In the evenings and off days, my dad waded through miles of paperwork. We needed insurance to cover the ranch, helmets to cover kid's heads, and a 501(c)3 to make us a legal nonprofit organization.

We brought in our church bus to serve as a tack room and gathered volunteers to help us with our dream. But that was still all it was: a dream.

Naming our dream also proved difficult. What could encompass all we planned and hoped and dreamed to do in the lives of the kids and families who would come through our gate? What name, when spoken, would bring a smile and a feeling of safety to those who would come? After much praying and hashing through options, my family named our dream: Sky View.

Despite all the work that we had done, Sky View was still just a name, a hope, insurance, horses, and helmets until the day I stepped into the arena with my first student. His mom had called me, a mother longing to see the best for her child. She desired to see him grow in confidence despite living in the confident shadow of his older brother. As we talked on the phone, I scheduled a time for him to come up and ride.

He stepped out of the car—a shy little boy in rubber boots. He would not make eye contact and any communication had to be dragged out of him. I began my first lesson, explained herd dynamics a little bit, talked about horse body language, then stepped with him into the arena to catch his horse. In that moment, an intangible dream—one that despite the insurance, the work, and the helmets seemed so far away—became reality. I watched the wonder of a small boy running his fingers over a horse. As he rode and fell in love with Sweet Grass's bold spots, an intangible dream became reality—a reality named Sky View.

Eleven

Worthy of Love

Amy's student was preparing for the worst when she asked, "So, what do I do if my saddle catches on fire?" She asked how to deal with the worst-case scenario; she needed to know for future planning. In working with horses over the years, I have seen many things happen, but never a saddle catching on fire. But to the little girl on the big horse's back, it was important to know what to do, if . . . She was ready, come what may. I have found that many of our students—many people—do that. They prepare for the worst-case scenario in life, but so often in doing that, they miss out on the very best. If we can be distracted by the "what if," we can lose focus on the "what is."

My student comes across as strong. Each time she steps out of her car at the ranch, she strides with confidence; she is bold in her conversation and overly confident in her horse skills. But she picked Simon as her horse—a horse that is not welcome in the herd he lives with. He is a bit of a social nerd and the other horses do not like him. He frequently gets lost and spends a lot of his time alone. In watching her come each week, I have seen why she chose Simon. She is a misfit too; many people do not like my little girl.

She struggles with relationships in school because, like Simon, she is smart, but comes across socially unskilled. She struggles with anger and it threatens to rear its ugly head at inopportune times in her life. On top of all of that, she is in foster care because of her mother. She lost the woman who is supposed to fight for her life, because she instead threatened it. Needless to say, the walls of protection she has built around her heart are thick and high. No one can enter. Over the course of life—through the pain—she has been taught to prepare for the worst. The "what if". . . ?

She sat astride Simon. She had had a hard week of running away, self-harm, police, and anger. Her foster mommy, who loves her mightily, sequestered herself in the car for some quiet while her daughter rode. I searched for words—what to say to a broken girl. Then as I was thinking, trying to start a conversation that would lead to something of importance, Simon reached over with his overly friendly mouth and tried for a little nibble on my arm. Through Simon's actions, God spoke. He gave clear direction on what she was doing, the reasons that I was struggling to build a relationship with her. After a moment's consideration and questioning, "God is that really it?" I went out on a limb and opened my mouth.

"Do you see how Simon tries to push me away by biting at me?" I heard a yes behind me, "Do you think it might be because he is so convinced that no one could love him that when people try, he reacts to them?" She thought about it and nodded. He did it again. I kept walking at his shoulder, then spoke to the girl behind me. "Is that what you are doing?" I turned in time to see her falsely confident eyes drop. "Are you so convinced that people are not going to love you that you push them away when they try?" She was listening, then nodded. My heart pounded in the realization of what God had revealed to me.

After a quiet moment, I heard a little, hard heart cry out, "No one has ever loved me." My heart broke. Her mother, the foster families she had been thrust into, and the life she had lived in her thirteen years had convinced her that she was unlovable. Oh if only she knew the love, most passionate, a life given in trade for hers—Jesus' blood shed on the cross. "Greater love has no man than this . . ." Jesus laid down His life for her . . . for the girl who had "never been loved."

So I told her of Jesus' love—a love so passionate, so beautiful, and all-encompassing. I explained the love I saw her new foster mom giving her—the reason they called the police when she ran away was because they loved her. And for a brief moment, a small, hurt little girl peeked out through a chink in her castle of pain. I thought she might be ready to take on the hurt, that I could show her the fullness of love. I watched as excruciating pain creased her face and flashed through her eyes. For a brief moment she was vulnerable, her lips trembled as she fought tears, then the door was slammed, the wall built higher, and she changed the subject. The "what if?" slammed the door, preparing for something as unfathomable as a saddle catching on fire. Sure that no one could love her, a girl whose name means "deserving of love" slammed the opening door on love. Life is safer without it . . .

Perfect

The girl stood in His presence
The road there had been rough
He looked at all she'd gone through
She'd never been enough

A weak and wounded damsel
The girl He'd come to save
As she stood there in His presence
Her walls began to cave

For she thought she felt His presence
Something more than life can give
Then she cried out in His presence
For she so longed to live

"If you're real would you please show me
Who on earth I am"
And so the King of Glory
Answered with a Lamb

He began to paint her life song
All covered by His death
And as the colors flourished
The world caught its breath

For it saw the girl so lovely
In a dress of purest white
And despite the times she'd failed
She was perfect in His sight

Twelve

Quiet Hands

A shaky breath was drawn, then a stylish black zippered boot slipped into the stirrup. I held her horse in the round pen. She mumbled, "I can do all things through Christ who strengthens me, Philippians 4:13," under her breath. Then she reached up and pulled herself into the saddle. She drew in another deep breath, lifted her reins and was ready. It was time to take her maiden voyage.

Watching Rosie sitting on Sweet Grass, you never would guess that when she had climbed on a horse for the first time a few short years before, fear had controlled the whole situation. At that time, sitting on a horse had been too much to take in. It so overwhelmed her that she had run. Throwing herself out of the saddle, she had run away from me and out of the round pen as fast as she could. She had wanted to ride so badly, but she found herself running away from the horse that drew her.

We do a lot of fear facing here at Sky View and Rosie's fear was no different. I had found what she was afraid of and now I needed her to face it so I could help her work through it. A lot of the kids that come here have fears that we work through, whether it be the fear of horses, the fear of being pushed outside one's comfort zone, or the fear of love.

As I talked Rosie back to the round pen, I realized we were dealing with far more than I had initially seen. On top of her struggle with cerebral palsy, there was an unexplainable fear and her default reaction was to run from it. The horses were especially overwhelming. Fortunately, the desire to ride a horse drew her like a magnet; she stepped back into the round pen and walked back up to the horse.

Rosie wrestled with her fear for a while; Sweet Grass stood. There was something different about this lesson and she waited patiently for her little rider to muster the courage to climb back into the saddle she had so recently fled from. She watched, reading her young student, with her feet planted. She was immovable for a short miraculous time. Rosie stood on the mounting block beside her; the moment had come. Her hands fluttered, the cerebral palsy reacting to the fear. Then I heard it, a soft word from her mother outside the round pen. "Rosie what is your verse?" She paused, and quoted her verse, "I can do all things through Christ who strengthens me, Philippians 4:13." I joined her and we said it again.

Then she slipped her boot into the stirrup and climbed on. The first steps of fear were conquered.

Over and over, she came back. The fear of climbing on was covered in the verse, "I can do all things through Christ who strengthens me, Philippians 4:13," and she did. For years, Rosie has come to the ranch every week all summer long. She faces each fear with her eyes closed and her verse quoted. Over time she has watched her brother excel at riding. Her younger sister has grown old enough to ride and has become a skilled little rider on Stripe, but Rosie has had to wait to hold the reins. She had yet another struggle to conquer.

Rosie's excitement was often displayed in her hands shaking. She would get overwhelmed and I would watch her hands come up shaking and flutter around her face for a time. Then she would regain control and they would settle back in her lap. The shaking was brought on, as far as I understood, by the cerebral palsy. Her mom told me that with work, she could control it. In the best interest of the horse and knowing the confusion that shaking reins would give the horse, I told her she had to be able to keep her hands still while she rode—excited or not. With holding the reins as her goal, she settled into working on controlling her hands.

As she mastered it, week after week, we led her around and around the arena. All the while, little things were conquered but her hands still fluttered. She rode, we talked, and we waited. Each time her nerves would work against her, I would watch her move her shaking hands to the saddle horn, wrap her fingers around it, and hold a white knuckle grip until she was back in control. Another step closer.

After two and a half years, I slipped the bit into Sweet Grass' mouth, buckled the throat latch, and clipped the rainbow reins onto the O ring of the snaffle bit. Rosie followed me up the hill, through the gate, and into the large round pen. We were back to where she had started, the arena she had fled from so many rides ago. She stood on the mounting block, Sweet Grass still beside her, and we quoted her verse, "I can do all things through Christ who strengthens me."

Then she slipped her boot into the stirrup and climbed on.

It was so like the first day, but unlike any ride she had had before, as I reached up and handed her reins. After two and a half years of waiting, we worked through the lesson that usually comes two or three weeks after a child first starts coming to the ranch. I directed her on how to turn Sweet Grass, how to guide her movement around the arena, and where to hold her hands. Small, still hands held Sweet Grass' reins as she moved her 1,000 pound horse around the small round pen. We reveled in victory.

She had conquered her ultimate goal—her hands were quiet; she had beat it. God had given her the strength to control her hands despite the cerebral palsy. So many of the conversations we had were in regards to God making her strong enough to handle the effects of the cerebral palsy, and she had done it. She had beat it; her reins had been earned. "I can do all things through Christ who strengthens me."

Several weeks later, summer was coming to a close. Rosie's family drove up to the ranch and life and enthusiasm climbed out of their van in the form of four kids. Siblings, looking for Chill, the cat, raced by me. Stories were exchanged and hugs given all around. They wanted to ride Erik, so we led him out of the pasture and saddled him up.

After her brother's lesson, we quoted her verse and Rosie mounted. It was time to let her trot. I clipped the red lunge line to Erik's bit and asked him to walk around me. Then, from the center, I stepped him up into a trot. Fear crossed her face and we worked through it. In a short time, he was trotting his heavy Haflinger trot around me and she was bouncing to the fluidity of his movement.

As he circled and circled me, she dropped her reins, rested her hands on her saddle, closed her eyes, and tipped her head back. Her raven black hair pulled back in a ponytail bounced and swayed to his trot. Watching her, no one would have guessed that the movement of a horse had crippled her with fear such a short time ago. They would only have seen a little girl, totally at peace with life, trotting a circle on a big horse with her eyes closed and a peaceful smile flashing in the sunlight.

HANNAH SWAYZE

*"No wonder Sweet Grass has patches—
she's trying to cover up her spots!"*

Kemakasa

The young Arab danced to the show ring
Flashily strutting her breed
And as her owner rode her
She was all that fame would need

For she had the conformation
The beauty and air of grace
And the treasure of her heritage:
Her softly dishing face

So she strode into the show ring
Her trot precise and clean
As she danced around the judges
In flowing spotless sheen

Then she stopped and held her head high
The judges took another look
As she posed so soft and elegant
They marked things in their book

Then they called out the winners
From 8th to 2nd place
She arched her neck and cameras flashed
As a blue was hung by her face

The sleek little bay took her victory lap
The honor of the blue
Raucous applause and camera flash
Marked the honor she so well knew

The years went by so quickly
Till the horse was old and thin
She stood beneath the spreading trees
Awaiting the day to begin

Then tires crunched up the driveway
Out stepped a girl with a freckled face
Her blonde hair bobbed in a ponytail
Every movement full of grace

She worked for her final decision
Then a pink halter led the way
For she'd spent the whole week deciding
Stripe would be her horse for the day

BELOVED

The horse greeted her so eager
Joy bubbled from deep inside
She awaited in expectation
Her eyes sparkled full and wide

Then grace climbed onto a graceful back
They danced the lesson's flight
Joyful bounce, ponytail bob
Complete in freedom's light

Then a blue was hung on her headstall
Blue eyes popped with honor's awe
For she'd won the badge of courage
Conquered the fear that no one saw

Then the little bay took her victory lap
The greatest she ever would stride
As a little girl who'd conquered her fear
Smiled the joy from deep inside

For Stripe,
Thank you for all the victory laps
you've taken our kids on. May your life hold
many more blues my little war horse.

Thirteen

Allured to the Wilderness

I watched as the beautiful, red roses died and fell from the vines. The leaves were withered too. It looked like I had killed the climbing roses my grandma had given me years before. It had been with their best intention in mind, that I had freed them from their potted cage on a warm early summer evening. I had high hopes of them climbing and bringing their red blossom beauty to the ranch, but it appeared that I had cut their little plant life short with my lack of gardening ability.

Each summer God gives me a passage of scripture to lean on during the long, hot days. The words speak of what I am going through. They also remind me of God's faithfulness so that I can trust Him with the beloved lives of my students. This year I was reading through the Minor Prophets when He spoke my summer passage.

"Therefore, behold, I will *allure* her,

Will bring her into the wilderness

and speak *comfort* to her.

I will give her her vineyards from there,

And the Valley of Achor as a door of *hope*;

She shall *sing* there, as in the days of her youth,

As in the day when she came

up from the land of Egypt."

Hosea 2:14-15

God's people had once again run after different gods. They had become well established in their lives and in their ways. They had turned their back on God, again, so He declared that He would strip them of what they knew. He said their vineyards, their livelihood, what they had come to depend on would all be taken away and through the alluring of the Most High God, they would enter the wilderness. He was willing to walk them through the wasteland, and the difficulty of need to bring them ever closer to His heart. He would reclaim their worship and dependency in the lonesomeness of the wilderness.

Years before I read this passage, God drew me nearer to Himself. The wilderness was dark, but the dependency on Jesus that it forced me to have is still glorious.

I will never forget the longing, the gnawing desire to have a horse. Growing up, our neighbor had a stunning dapple gray Arabian gelding that lived right across the fence. My dream of owning a horse was separated by the great expanse of a woven wire fence. He was so close I could even touch him at times, but he was not mine, so I wept. I clearly remember standing in our pasture crying out to God the sorrows of a little girl's heart, praying for a horse of my own.

Then it all came true. As we drove home one late Christmas Eve, my dad asked what I wanted for Christmas. I smiled sleepily and whispered out my desire for a horse. The next morning, the prayer that I had cried out to God in the privacy of our pasture and the darkness of the gift-filled car was answered. On a clear Christmas day, our neighbors led a beautiful chestnut mare, with a flaxen mane and tail, down our driveway and into my heart. She was the embodiment of a dream and many tearful prayers of a young girl's heart. Her name was Sarah.

For six beautiful years, she walked hoofprints through my life. She was my taste of freedom, wings after a long day of school, and the best friend an insecure teen could ever find. I spent hours brushing her chestnut color to a gloss, riding her, barefoot and bareback, through the moonlight and sharing my heart with her small, listening ears.

Then on June 10th of 2005, I rode her before I left on a mission trip. As I rode, I felt her passion had slowed. Something felt different as I said goodbye and three days later, a part of my heart died when I got the call. She had lain down in the warmth of a summer afternoon and had died. My wilderness started on the top of the back corner bunk of the dorm I was sharing with several girls. I curled up on my bed and wept the pain of a shattered heart.

All that week I broke, but I found the hoofprints Sarah had walked into my soul led me to the foot of Jesus. In the lonely wilderness of sorrow, I realized that she had been number one in my life. She was my closest friend, my security, and the one I shared my heart with. As God, jealous for my heart, reclaimed lordship in my life, Sarah's hoofprints ended and Jesus took my hand to lead me deep into His love.

Over the last few days of the mission trip, God enthroned Himself in my life. Sarah could no longer be number one in importance. Despite a broken heart, God proved His faithfulness over and over and over to me. In the wilderness I found the oasis of His love. He established Himself as God, Lord of my life, and shelter in the storm. Through Sarah, my answer to prayer and gift of God, He had led me to a place of falling deeper in love with the King of my heart.

When I returned home, in the pasture where I was usually greeted with the love and warmth of my little Arabian, I was met with a pile of fresh dirt cascading with roses. I lay in the moist dirt and sobbed—great, alone, wilderness sobs. When I arose a long time later, I continued on the journey with my King.

In the wildernesses of my heart, God continually proves Himself. As my eyes meet those of the people who come to the ranch, I frequently see the lonely eyes of those lost in the desolation of needing a Savior. They long to find the oasis, the answers, and so Hosea spoke to me as I read. When I look at people who come, I so often want to do the alluring: to show kids and families how amazing a life of serving God can be . . . but God does the alluring. The sweet drawing call can only be spoken by the God of all creation, the One who died to make the calling of value. I cannot draw students into the love of God. He does.

The roses from my grandma had sat for years in pots, waiting for their move into their forever home. I had always put it off because my family was planning on moving. Once we moved to Sky View, I was leery to plant them where the deer might eat them. Then in the business of life, I had forgotten them (yes, I am terrible with plants). When I finally noticed them, I dug their pots out of the grass that had grown up around them and took them down to the tack room on the back of the four-wheeler.

I cut through the plastic flowerpot and was shocked to find that there was hardly room for dirt. The roots had grown so thick, and I felt a twinge of guilt as I dug the hole for them. After coaxing them out of the pot, I embedded them in the dry summer soil.

After nestling them deep in the dirt and pouring water around them, I walked away. Visions of climbing red roses filled my mind and I was excited for them to flourish. A few days later the visions began to fade as the roses appeared to die. Flowers that had been alive wilted and fell to the ground. Leaves turned yellow and spotty and then also joined the petals with gravity's pull. It was a lost cause; I had killed them.

As I watched my roses wilt and die, I thought of the wildernesses God calls us into sometimes—areas where we are totally at a loss and desperately in need of Him. We often meet our ranch families in the driest, darkest hour of their wandering. I meet them there in the dry blowing dirt and think, what on earth do I have to offer them? His answer: comfort. He promises to speak comfort.

It is beautiful, as I walk out my desire to be the hands and feet of Jesus. I have comfort to offer in the pain of the wilderness. Then, as God begins to give His people back, through Him, what He has taken away, He offers hope—a hope far sweeter than the life lived before the wilderness.

It seemed foolish to water the dead looking sticks of what had once been a thriving bush, but I did (when I remembered). I poured buckets of water on the dry ground around my grandma's gift in hopes that maybe I had not completely killed them. Then one day, as I looked closely, I saw life—hope. There were new leaves growing where the last ones had died and fallen. Hope kindled, in the soft green of new life.

Such a similar hope we have to offer. In the driest of the wildernesses, we have the hope, the "water" to see them through because we know the Savior, who is the ultimate hope.

BELOVED

"I've ridden an English and a Western saddle, but never a French one."

Fourteen

Go into All the World

There were no chairs, so we sat on the wood floor of the tack room. The workday was complete and we were bringing our day to a close. Stud walls reached eight feet closer to the sky around us as I sat with my back against a new wall. Without a ceiling yet, light filtered through the floor joists of what would someday be the second floor. Our saddle rack and everything we needed on a daily basis for lessons was stashed under a tarp in the middle of the room. Our group sat in the middle of the chaos: a construction zone.

Around the clutter on the floor, our group of faithful volunteers prayed over the new room we sat in—for those who would enter and the part that these simple walls would play in the work on the ranch. Then, curled against the wall, I began to sing.

"My Jesus, my Savior, Lord there is none like you." A choir of voices grew around me as we initiated the tack room with one of my favorite songs. "All of my days I want to praise the wonders of your mighty love." In the chaos of construction, we sang of the wonders of God, who He was, and the work He was going to do within those walls. "My comfort, my shelter, tower of refuge and strength; let every breath, all that I am, never cease to worship You." He would be the comfort, the strength to be and do all that He called us to. So we moved to worship and sought the joy of giving Him all that we are.

"Shout to the Lord, all the earth, let us sing. Power and majesty, praise to the King. Mountains bow down and the seas will roar at the sound of Your name. I sing for joy at the work of your hands, forever I'll love You, forever I'll stand. Nothing compares to the promise I have in You."

God says to go into all the world to preach the gospel. Shout to the Lord, all the earth. But I have found at Sky View, sometimes the world comes to us. They walk through our gates and we get to share with them the promise that we have—hope, salvation, peace, and redemption. Recently, thirteen boys from all over the world walked into Sky View's world. They came to the ranch, pitched tents up on the hill and camped there for a time. They spent their days playing, eating, and visiting the Molalla River to cool off.

They were a group of boys made up mostly of refugees. They had all fled their countries, for whatever reason, at different times and had been moved to an apartment complex in Portland. The leaders of the camping trip were men who went to a church close to where the boys lived. They had committed to reaching out to the boys and their families, and in doing that, took them camping annually.

The day we arranged with their leaders for the boys to ride finally came. It was a huge task to let that many kids ride in a short amount of time and staff and volunteers prepared together to make the most of our time. When the time came to ride, boys wandered down the driveway from their campsite. We stepped out of a completed tack room to greet them. As kids from all over the world stepped through the door of the tack room, the prayer that we had sung so many months ago was continuing to be answered.

Through the chatter of broken English, I told them that they all needed closed-toed shoes and a helmet if they were going to ride. Socks were borrowed, boots pulled out of the boot bin and tried on, and helmets were fitted over dark hair.

Audrey saddled Satin and headed to the big round pen. I grabbed Erik and positioned myself in the small sandy round pen. Thirteen boys, with white helmets and borrowed boots, stood along the corral gates and edges. Cell phones were pulled out to document the occasion as the first boy climbed on.

I asked him if he had ever ridden a horse. He nodded then informed me that the last horse that he had ridden was in Syria—a world away.

He was delighted by the feel of Erik's muscular frame moving under him. As I led Erik around the round pen, a smile split the dark skin of his face. He moved with the fluidity of Erik, bareback and without hesitation. We talked, as we walked circles around the arena. His friends heckled him, when I led Erik up into a slow trot around the round pen. The laughter of many boys, including the one on Erik's back, filled the air.

Boy after boy climbed on as the time progressed—each one from a different culture. Some boys quiet and reserved, others boldly confident. Young men from all over the world described their languages, cultures, and religions to me, as I led them around the round pen. I reveled in the time, as each boy stepping through the gate brought with him a new country, culture, or language. We were touching the world, one little boy at a time.

All the staff did their part. Volunteers talked with the kids who were not riding. Audrey laughed with her riders in the big round pen and the ranch buzzed with life, as boys threw apples to the horses, laughed over riding, and played with the big bubble mixture that someone had given us.

Then another young man stepped into the round pen. I began to talk to him, explaining to him how to get onto Erik and was faced with a blank stare. He had only been in America for a short time. I stood in the round pen with the half-ton horse, Erik, and a young man unable to communicate through simple words. His friend stepped in to save us and began translating for me. They were both from the Middle East, so their languages were close enough to carry on conversation. Through words that meant nothing to my ears, his eyes lighted and he suddenly knew what I was telling him. He nimbly mounted the horse, gave me the universal thumbs up that he was enjoying it, and rode. It was incredible.

Of the thirteen boys who came, there were nine different languages spoken, not counting English. The boys had names I could not pronounce and spoke in languages I had never even heard of. It was an amazing experience. After they rode Erik, they would run to Satin or vice versa. Each one smiled and enjoyed the ride for the first time or at least for the first time in America. When they were done riding, they helped throw apples to the other horses in the corral.

Volunteers in Michael Jordan sandals and socks—for their boots were the borrowed ones—walked around monitoring the chaos, playing with bubbles, and handing out apples to throw. After all the boys were done riding and they were sorting who owned what shoes, I had each boy put a dot on his home country on my world map. Some smeared a dot on their country while others took time, almost seeming to look for a familiar tree by their old home before carefully placing the dot.

I look at my map. Go into all of the world? What if they come to you? What if you need a translator to explain to them how to jump up on the horse? The love of God that flows here transcends all the languages that walked Sky View that day. And laughter flowed. Laughter and love need no translation.

"Shout to the Lord all the earth let us sing, power and majesty praise to the King . . ."

Fifteen

Open to Linger

My uncle Mel is a master craftsman. Anything he puts his mind to is built with a few strokes of his skilled fingers. Simple wood takes on unique design and beauty through his touch, metal is fashioned into shapes no one knew it contained and it takes breaths away. This man has built everything from a sail boat to a ring made out of a walnut. His creations decorate walls, shelves, and kitchens all over the place.

In watching him work, I am honored to see how much he values what his nieces and nephews are doing. He has put hours of time into helping me with things for the ranch. He has done everything from building our saddle racks and pounding nails in the tack room to building me up and encouraging me in my walk with the Lord and in the ministry I am doing.

One of my favorite of my uncle's creations is a big door. It separates the tack room from the rest of the ranch. It is thick and heavy. The width is far bigger than a saddle ever will be and the latch is easy to open while carrying all the things necessary for working with horses.

My uncle designed it especially for the needs of the ranch. He came and measured a hole in the wall of the tack room and left with measurements scratched on a card. A few days later he returned with our door. As he hung the beautiful door on the thick, sturdy hinges, I laid my hands on the rough wood and prayed.

As he worked, I prayed that all who entered through the door would find refuge and linger, with the weight of the world set aside to simply dwell. Through the noise of the drill, I prayed blessing on all who entered in. I prayed that people would come through the door and stay long enough to leave rested, blessed by the love of God.

Every day at the ranch, when I am done reading my Bible, I unlock and swing the door wide. It stands open, ready to welcome all who would enter. God has answered my prayer. All through the day, I find students, parents, and volunteers scattered around the room. They linger over a conversation, a coloring book, or a game and all who pass through the door-way are reluctant to leave. There is a desire to stay, to dwell in the oasis of refuge, like sitting at the table after a good meal. All day long people sit and bask in the love that they stepped into when they walked through our open door.

"Dear Lord, I pray that Erik not be a snot and that he listens to me."

Sixteen

Beth

The fragrance of God is constantly being diffused here at Sky View. We lay before our families a feast—a feast of God's love, His redemptive forgiveness and His desire to see their lives restored. We cannot force them to take part in the meal any more than you can make a horse drink water, but we lay it before them nonetheless. I grieve often as I watch starving people come to the ranch, thrive in the sweetness of His love, then walk away from the feast, the promise of an abundant life, because they are so unsure of their Creator and the love that He has for them.

There surely must be a catch; the feast cannot be free. It is true the feast is not free; the cost of being a bond servant is a life of servanthood, but His service is never more than we can handle. What they do not seem to realize is that they are serving someone. By making the choice to not serve Jesus, they are in turn serving His enemy, whose main goal is to steal, kill, and destroy as many of God's creations as he can.

Yet they balk at serving their Creator—a God who loves them far more than they can realize. These parents come to the ranch seeking help for their kids because they love them. I wonder sometimes if they fully realize how valuable they are; that God gave His Son in exchange for them. Their salvation was worth death on a cross. They are redeemed; they just have to choose to step into that redemption and change masters—from serving a wicked master, Satan, and the sin he encompasses, to serving Jesus and the sweet love that He embodies.

Beth's grandparents were at a loss. Their little granddaughter was slipping away a little bit more each day. The alcohol and drugs that had surged through her system before birth had forever altered much of her reasoning power. She was following in the footsteps of her mother and they had done everything they could think of to help her. Her church family loved her, they cared about her, and taught her the truth of God, but she slowly strayed further and further away.

She soon became a part of my life as she started coming for lessons. She had ridden some before, at a safe house she had lived in for a time and I heard many stories of the horses she loved. I got to know her as we shared laughter, tears, and hearts. I listened to her for hours as she processed life from the back of a horse. I mentored her, gave godly insight into situations and prayed for her. Her hugs were willing and given freely. Life had hurt and she was thriving on having a friend who cared about her with no strings attached. I was willing to give her friendship without asking anything in return.

Every chance I got, I showed Beth the sweetness of God's love in her life. She was thriving on it at the ranch, but at home things continued to crumble. There was so much hurt in her past and so many struggles she faced that life was too much. So she ran—and that set a pattern. She would run, someone would hurt her in incomprehensible ways and she would come back to the ranch broken, hurting and in desperate need of a hug. I would hug her, help her saddle her horse and she would ride and talk.

I have found over the course of working with children that horses lead to good conversations. There is something about being on the back of a horse. I cannot explain it, but there is a freedom to talk about life from the safety of a saddle. Kids who would hesitate to open up about what they are thinking about from the ground are willing to share their heart with me from the height of a horse.

Beth's life was a cycle of hurt and pain, lost ground, and sorrow. Then one day, she was up on her favorite horse riding and talking. We were talking about the voices that she was hearing, telling her to run. I asked her whose voice she thought it was. She was not sure. So I asked if she thought God would tell her to run and do things that would hurt her. She said no. The only other option was the devil, who was once again seeking to kill and steal and destroy a life created by God.

She mentioned something about trying to be a good Christian, so I asked her what she thought a Christian looked like. She described a relationship of works. I had her stop her horse and looked her in the eyes and told her that she could never be good enough to go to Heaven. God sent His Son, who was the only One good enough to pay the price for sin. In Jesus' sacrificial death and resurrection, He made a way for us to have our sins forgiven. All we have to do is ask for Him to forgive us and make Him Lord of our life.

She thought about that. I asked Beth if she had ever done that before. She shook her head but said she would like to. I explained to her how to pray—the simple act of talking to God to forever alter the course of her eternity. Sweet Grass stood, quiet and still, as I watched one of God's creations pray and accept the free gift of forgiveness for a life of sin. She gave up ownership and allowed the Lord of Creation to become Lord of her life. It was glorious. Her radiant smile met mine as she opened her eyes.

Later I heard her tell her grandpa what had happened and we all joined the angels in their rejoicing.

Seventeen

Imitation

Awhile back, I was at the annual Hoedown for Crystal Peaks Youth Ranch, the ministry that we have patterned Sky View after, in many ways. It was exciting to see where Sky View could potentially be, years down the road. They have been open for many years and have had a great impact on their community. I stood in the middle of the chaos, doing one of my favorite things: people watching. I observed children laughing on the swing, families getting their picture taken and an older gentleman teaching small children the art of throwing a nice loop with a lariat. The potato gun was blasting apples out into the horse field and laughter conveyed the festive harvest feeling.

As I watched one of the staff guys walk by, there was a small boy right at his hip—a little shadow. While they were walking by, the boy looked up into the face of the man he was shadowing. Delighted to be by his side in anticipation of all that would come, the thrill of being with a man he looked up to—the look was one of adoration and mere words cannot fully explain the power of a young man's look of admiration toward the man he wants to be like. It struck me with a smile. Then I began to think about how our program does not have any guy instructors. None of our guy volunteers were eighteen—the age our insurance requires to teach a lesson. I looked forward to the day that they "age in" and can mentor the kids while doing lessons.

My students usually arrive at a quiet peaceful ranch on lesson days. They drive up to find me standing in an empty parking lot surrounded by pasture, trees, an arena, love, and silence. Laughter soon rings out alongside the melody of saddles, bridles, horses, and life. Through it all, they rarely ever notice directly the changes of their sweet haven: bark dust is simply spread, weeds are pulled, fences changed, and all the while buildings rise steadily to the height of their full potential. The students usually just see the beauty of their adventure.

I have the privilege of knowing those who make the subtleties happen. Once a month, an army of volunteers converges on Sky View with the purpose of making it lovely. They take tasks that would take me weeks to do on my own and simply complete them. Laughter and accomplishment rule the day as they seek to bless me, the ranch, the kids, and each other. I usually hand them a list that seems to be many feet long and they complete it in a few hours.

These teens are mission-minded. They have a desire to serve their King and they put that into action by blessing the ranch. Oftentimes I watch them work and see the people whom God has sent me. They joke, laugh, tease, and work in T-shirts, jeans, and rubber boots. They bring everything that they could possibly need to make the jobs that I give them better. The tack room is full of backpacks containing knives, lunches, ropes, machetes, and swim suits for the river swim when we are done and anything else that they think they could possibly need.

I step back between giving direction and watch as soldiers converge upon the ranch—men and women, serving as the hands and feet of their King. They do all that they do for His glory and it blows my mind. I do not think they realize the power behind their actions. Only a few of them wear actual camouflage, but all of them have made the decision to enlist in the service of their God.

I am always humbled to watch as they take miserable jobs, smile, and work through them with excellence. One of the days we were working, I talked with Corey, who has been working at the ranch for years. I mentioned that it was hard for me to have to give them all the tasks that I did not have time or ability to do. He looked at me and told me, "Hannah, we do what we do so that you can do what you do." They view their work as enabling me to do what I am called to do. Through their work, they are touching the lives of the kids.

God sends me soldiers who will help me fix fences and keep the ranch looking so wonderful as an encouragement. They are too young in the eyes of our insurance to do the work of teaching lessons, so they enable me to teach by freeing me of so many responsibilities. God has a way of upholding the arms of His people by sending other soldiers to lift them in their fight. Someday I pray these teenage warriors will see how mighty they are in upholding the work at Sky View.

Grant is one of our faithful volunteers. He has been coming up and helping with workdays for years. He has sweat, bled, and killed many weeds for the sake of Sky View. When I asked him if he wanted to help with the kid interaction portion of the ministry, his eyes lit up and he agreed to help. Each year he has grown more and the boy I used to look down at physically has become a man spiritually and surpassed me in height as well.

This year he took on an even greater role in ranch leadership and the lessons. I purposely pair him with the young men who have come up to ride. He works side by side with the girls, giving lessons so that the boys have a man they can spend time with and look up to. In our mentoring, I wanted him to be the one that the boys he worked with looked up to and would want to pattern their life after.

He has done an excellent job and has far surpassed all of my expectations. It really had not hit me until we were all at Sky View's open house, eating our lunch. We were sitting with our students and Grant had one of "his" young men shouldered up to him. As we talked and ate, I watched as they were visiting and Grant did something to make him laugh. My student looked at Grant with the sparkle of admiration. He was sitting beside a man, his friend, and also a man that he would want to be like.

My throat felt thick as I watched a dream fulfilled. Here I had thought that we were lacking, because we did not have men directly teaching lessons. But looking around our open house, there was an army of men—though teenagers in the world's eyes—worthy of admiration, respect, and shadowing. These men had won the right to influence so many boys— such a hard-earned honor. I stepped back and marveled over God's provision. Through the years, these young volunteers have worked with, mentored, and built these young men up in the Lord. The mentoring that happens at Sky View goes so far. The lives being changed by lives committed to serving God.

Mire

The girl floundered in the mire
The constant muck of the world
She wandered through the valleys
Trying to see through all that was hurled

She knew her Maker had a plan
And worked to see His hand
But while she slogged on lonely
She longed for Heaven's land

For the world's weight was crushing
Far more than she could bear
And the wounds and hurts of life
Daily seemed to tear

For she did not see the angels
The strength when she was weak
As she trudged on through the valley
And waited to hear Him speak

Then her King softly reminded
To look to Him with all her might
With Him her only focus
Everything would be alright

Eighteen

Holy, Holy, Holy . . .

The day's work was done. I stepped out of the tack room door for the last time. The lock clicked, and I was finished. The phone calls were made, the meetings met, and the horses wormed. As I closed the door, the song *Holy, Holy, Holy! Lord God Almighty!* was on my mind. I sang it as I looked at the sunset over Sky View. Dinner was calling.

God has a way of calling louder. I was allured to linger. I drifted toward the day's work: the beginnings of the pole barn indoor riding arena. The posts jutted toward the sky at awkward angles as they sat in the holes. I began to pray, "Holy, holy, holy, Lord God Almighty."

I prayed for the newest Sky View building. While laying hands on the rough, pressure-treated post, I prayed for all who would enter—peace, refuge, and that God would meet people in the confines of those walls. I prayed for safety as we rode and walked my first laps in prep for walking alongside a student. Holy, holy, holy, Lord God Almighty ran through my mind. The posts leaned in.

In the book of Revelation, John shares his vision of heaven with us. There are four creatures who, day and night, say, "Holy, holy, holy, Lord God Almighty, Who was and is and is to come." Each time it's said, there are 24 elders who fall down before the throne of God. Holy, holy, holy, Lord God Almighty.

When I was done praying over the new building, I continued walking. Students' names came to mind as I walked, so I prayed over them as I journeyed across the familiar path around the arena. Then something caught my eye as my shadow fell on a trail—a trail worn into the dirt by Stripe as she walked the arena all winter.

The trail zigged and zagged, showing where the muddiest spots were avoided and the footing was best. My shadow fell on the crooked path as I prayed. A favorite verse came to mind: "Your ears shall hear a word behind you, saying, 'This is the way, walk in it,' whenever you turn to the right hand or whenever you turn to the left." Isaiah 30:21.

I prayed for our students—the lives of kids we would touch as they came to ride. I prayed they would be directed to the straight and narrow—that they would hear God's voice directing them in their way. That through the impact of our touching their lives, they will fall at the feet of their Maker, knowing He is the only way, crying out in worship, Holy, holy, holy, Lord God Almighty.

Beyond the Gilding

Today I saw your Bible
So crisp and white and clean
As you marveled o'er its newness
The gilded pages' subtle sheen

You gently flipped the pages
So little clue for all they hold
The answer to every heart cry
And the way to the city of gold

You softly fondle the pages
With dreams of all they contain
As you slowly get to know it
I pray that you'll remain

I pray you'll look past the gilded pages
To the romance and thrill of living
That you'll fall in love with the Author
And be filled with a heart of giving

I pray that the crisp clean pages
Grow crinkled by loving hands
And wisdom be readily found
To meet the world's high demands

I pray that the pages are tear-stained
From a heart that's broken with pain
Finding refuge in the Lover
For in Him sorrow leads to gain

I pray that it becomes a friend
To correct and love and delight
That you can see you're standing
Enrobed in the purest white

That you'll see it never fails
But remains faithful to the end
That you can stand up to the trials
In the courage it will lend

I pray in the gilded pages
You'll find the gentle sweet love of His grace
And that you'll grow to know the Savior
As you meet Jesus face to Face

"Do you teach all your students to post so they don't give your horses a headache?"

Nineteen

The Softening of a Heart

Every time I corrected her, she would shut down. I would watch as a happy young girl would come to the ranch excited to see her horse. We would saddle and get ready, then the horse would misbehave so I would tell her how to fix the problem and she would resent it. Her eyes would drop, she would be frustrated by the fact that I needed to correct her, and she would allow that frustration to make her movements harsh to her horse. Most weeks were the same. She was annoyed that she could not get the Disney-perfect relationship between her and her horse and I would watch her respond as if I had physically hurt her every time I tried to direct her and help her with her horse.

Kaitlyn often left the ranch giving me my required hug in a stiff, distracted, and discouraged way. She was so motivated by her accomplishments that she did not want to need my help. Needless to say, she did not respond well to me. She would reject my instruction out of frustration and I would end each lesson feeling a greater distance and more frustration than when we started.

So I tried different approaches. Eventually, I ran out of ideas. I asked my dad for advice on the student who was not teachable and he gave me his thoughts. They crashed and another lesson ended badly; I was ready to quit.

The summer sun rose and I faced another lesson day with my un-teachable student. I honestly dreaded trying to show her my love when she took my corrections, that were for her safety, as her failure. It seemed like she was feeling threatened by me and wanted to prove herself, but could not make the horse be perfect. So I walked to work. I carried my bag and walked the lower fence line down to the ranch from where we live. The nice thing about your house being a half-mile from the main ranch is that walking to work gives you lots of time to think and pray and ask for wisdom.

As I prayed my way to the ranch on a warm morning, God laid it out for me. He showed me exactly what to do and my goal in doing it was to make her fail. He wanted me to set Kaitlyn up in an impossible situation. He made it clear to put her in the round pen with her horse and ask her to do some ground work. I knew that with her skill level, she would not be able to do what I was going to ask of her. She was sure to fail.

Before Kaitlyn and her family drove up the driveway, I practiced in the round pen. I asked the horse to do the highly improbable. She was unfamiliar with what I was asking of her. God confirmed His instruction when she surprised me by the horse doing exactly what I asked of her very well. I had never lunged her before and she did it as if we had practiced it a thousand times. I scratched her ears as they pulled into the driveway and whispered to her the plan of not doing it for my student. I needed her to fail.

Kaitlyn came, we hugged, and I told her that we were starting with ground work. I explained that I wanted her to plant her feet in the middle of the round pen, send her horse away from her into a circle around the edge, have her walk a few circles and then bring her back in. For a horse that had, to my knowledge, never been lunged, this was highly improbable.

I stepped out of the round pen, sat on my rock and watched. She worked and worked, trying different ideas and failing at all of them. Each time she asked the horse to move away, the horse would turn and look at her, confused by her directions. I kept quiet as she struggled. I was waiting for her to want my help. She fought on.

Finally, after a long while of trying I watched her body language; she gave up. I stood up and asked her, "Do you want my help?" She nodded. I prayed; now I needed the horse to listen again. I stepped into the middle and sent her off. She looked at me, turned, and walked a circle. It was beautiful.

Then I began to share. The words that came out of my mouth were spoken by God; this was His plan after all. As I worked the horse on the line, she did something wrong and I had to correct her. As I corrected her, I explained that if I ever want her to be more than a pretty pasture ornament I had to correct her. She had to be pushed and worked if she was ever going to amount to anything. Did it make her a horrible horse to have to be corrected? No, it just meant that she did not know the right way to do it yet. I needed to teach her some things and she became a better horse each time she took my correction; she learned.

I cued her and my horse turned in to look at me.

I then transferred that to my student. "Like this beautiful horse, I want you to reach your full potential as a horsewoman. If I correct you, it does not mean I hate you or that you have failed." I explained that I correct the horses because I care about them and want them to reach their full potential. God does the same thing with us. He sees our full potential and corrects us and changes us in order to make us into the people that He sees we can be. Sometimes He uses people to change and correct us. "I see what you could do and want to help you reach it."

I conveyed to her that I want to help her learn. When she asks me for help it does not mean I think she is a horrible person. I told her I want to be approachable and for her to know I am willing to help her.

I cued and the horse changed direction.

After a bit more ground work and talking, we saddled her horse and I let her ride. A soft hand and willing ears led to a wonderful lesson. We made it farther that lesson than we had on many lessons combined. Her hug was soft at the end.

From then on, lessons where pleasant. Horse and rider were gently corrected and things went far more smoothly. My beautiful student was willing to talk to me and we shared much laughter and horse time. A few weeks after I challenged her to take my correction a young girl who had been hesitant to let me into her life climbed out of her car with full eyes and snuggled into my arms. I held her, sobbing out her rough week, for a long time as I marveled at God's hand. I had set Kaitlyn up to fail with her horse and in exchange had gained a sweet, soft relationship.

Tarnished

She came up filth-encrusted
Tarnished black by the world's sin
Fallen victim to such harlotries
The appraise of men to win

She'd given herself so willingly
His attentions had been sought
And the remorse that briefly flickered
Was only guilt that they'd been caught

She came and walked beside me
Shoulder to shoulder to her grime
All I know is to simply love her
Be much more than a sounding chime

But the time with the filth and the dirty
Leaves me muddied by the weight of her loss
And all I can do with the burden
Is crawl to the foot of the cross

And lay at the foot of my Jesus
A burden that's so hard to bear
Knowing He sees me forgiven
And will mend every broken heart tear

Twenty

Meth and a Love Story

Life is a love story—and like all love stories it begins, "Once upon a time."

Once upon a time there was love, true love. God, holy and perfect, created—the making of something from absolute nothing. Dust became alive—so alive that it walked, talked, and breathed. But dust when it contains life can become lonely so God saw fit to make Adam a helpmate. Adam was put into a deep sleep, a rib was removed, and another life was formed out of the flesh.

Adam and Eve, the first people who walked with God; the beginning of the most beautiful love story.

The Creator was wise and knew that for His creation to truly love Him, they had to have a choice. He created life, not bodies that He could control. So dust—living flesh—was given a choice: live, thrive, and dwell in the relationship with

God. Or die. Disobedience and sin would lead to a decision that would forever alter the course of life and in the end lead to death—total separation from God. With free choice, His creations were free—free to serve Him or walk away from that love and forever end what they knew as life.

Love and life in Him were perfect, but for true love to really work, there always seems to be an enemy to contrast the goodness and love of the lover. Enter Satan—evil in every sense of the word. His vendetta against God stemmed from his own rebellion. He had wanted to be as God in Heaven. So he challenged the authority of God. He fell and one third of the angels with him. They were cast from Heaven—from the very presence of God.

Satan lost the battle against the Most High God. God wins.

Seeing that he could not bring harm to the King of kings, he sought to make His creation fall. Temptation came to Eve in the Garden of Eden. Despite her perfect relationship with God, she was drawn away by the promise that she could do better than God. She was convinced that He had withheld something from her and that by eating the fruit she could become like God. She picked it and the course of life was altered forever. Adam then ate of the forbidden tree and the Bible says that through one man, sin entered the world.

Through the sin came separation. The course of life was forever altered and remains altered for eternity. Because of Adam and Eve, all of mankind is tainted. Despite His passionate, unfailing love for all of humanity, we cannot stand in the perfection of His presence.

Revenge had found its first victim as Satan sought to kill, steal, and destroy our relationship with God. Revenge still wreaks havoc in the lives of the students who walk through our gate. We see the creation, desperately loved by their Creator, listening to the lies of Satan. The lie of his holding something better than God has been hissed through the ages, as people fall victim to the lies, deceit, and wretchedness of what sin claims to offer.

I peeked over a horse's back. Deep brown eyes welled like pools in her dark skin. They flashed beauty, the signs of a perfect creator. Her olive skin was framed by raven-black hair that shone in the sunlight. The marks of God's fingerprints were relevant in her face; she was lovely. Her laugh lilted over the back of her horse as we groomed and prepared to saddle.

While we brushed, we visited. We got along well and spent our lesson time laughing, telling stories, and talking. I worked, as I always do, to incorporate my love for Jesus into each conversation with my students, challenging them in hopes of leading them to the One who repaired the divide that was placed between them and their Creator.

I watched as the deceiver held her bound by so many lies. Scars on her arms denoted what she had believed and tried to relieve with physical pain. Makeup was heavy in hopes of taking the beauty that I saw and making it different to live up to the world's unreachable standards.

She was losing. Her boyfriends were not filling the empty need and nothing was working. I prayed that she would hit rock bottom soon so that she would be ready to hear of the redemption of Jesus. But each time I thought we reached the bottom it would drop out, deeper, in her attempts to relieve the emptiness.

"You did it again?" Dark eyes met mine. Nothing faltered as she responded with a yes. "Why did you do it?" I was shocked. We had dealt with drugs. It was normal. They were simple to get and easy to take. The comfort they offered was another way of masking her need for a deep personal relationship with her Savior. The deceiver had held up another piece of "forbidden fruit," something that seemed better and she had willingly bit.

But meth—that was a different story. She had tried it and hated it. She had told me in a previous lesson that it was wicked—the devil's drug—and that she would never take it again. When I asked her why she had tried it she shrugged, "I was curious." Her resolve to never take it again held for a short time, then it fell with a crash. Her desire had been indulged.

As with all of our students, Satan's hatred of God's greatest creation is evident. So many of our students come to the ranch with parents' marriages ending in divorce, their innocence stolen by a man in their life, or scars from trying to relieve emotional pain with cutting. Destruction is evident as Sky View opens its gates to the world. It is clear that there is an enemy, as so many hurt and wounded stumble through our gates in search of something that the devil cannot offer.

They come, hungry for hope and we have it. Through the cross, Jesus repaired the damage that was done so many years ago by Adam and Eve. He is the Redeemer; the Hero of the love story. The One who can save us from our sin. He died, sinless in our place because of His deep love for us. Redemption is offered. A gift, free for the taking. All that is required is a willingness, a heart repentant, humbled, ready to ask for the forgiveness that stands extended to all mankind.

In that moment, childhood is re-established. Rightstanding with God, is found as sins are forgiven and life in Christ Jesus' death is freely given. Hope. Freedom from the evil. Refuge to be found in the arms of the Most High.

After seeing the pain ravaged by the enemy and seeing the defiant eyes that had so recently been dulled by Meth; I could step back from a day and feel like the battle is lost. She ends up walking through the doors of a rehab center and the story ends in hopelessness. All our work at the ranch is useless, but then I step into my office and there in the corner is a cross, the defeat of the enemy. Apart from the hope of the blood shed on the cross, I have nothing to offer. So I simply relinquish control and linger at the feet of the One who died in my place; there is no sweeter refuge.

Suicide

Today I met with suicide
I looked it in the face
And with a small adventure
Brought laughter in its place

I helped it crawl up on a horse
Watched it stroke the winter hair
And as it sat there talking
It dwelt in the peace that was there

Then we built great castles
Crystal ice from hoof's round print
Acting as moats and guarded walls
Brought imagination's subtle glint

Then the horse was left to stand
As suicide followed me up the hill
We were off to explore a frozen land
An adventurous need to fill

HANNAH SWAYZE

I introduced it to a puddle
And ice rink, frozen, grand
And with shrieks of delighted pleasure
I led suicide out by the hand

And we skated as carefree children
In a land where no one could see
As adventure worked its purpose
I watched suicide filled with glee

Then we went back to her mother
The light of life in her eye
With God's love, some joy and adventure
Was there really a reason to die?

— Hannah Swayze

"Hannah, I tucked my shirt in just for you!"

Twenty-One

A Life Worth Living

Her mom called me, near tears. Her daughter was slipping farther and farther out of her grasp. She did not know what to do as she watched her daughter retreat further and further into herself. School was not attended, life was not engaged and family was avoided. Then it all broke. She had another run-in with the painful words of her dad and it all crashed.

Mom was sleeping quietly when she was shaken awake. Her daughter looked at her through the darkness. Fear flashed in her eyes. Poison control had told her to wake her mom and get to the hospital. The handful of pills she had swallowed would soon take effect and shut down her liver. Suicide was scary and she had come to her mother for help. The lie she had been told, freedom in death, came at a high price.

They rushed to the hospital, her stomach was pumped, and life continued. I got the phone call and heard the mom's overwhelmed version of the story. They were coming to the ranch to ride and she had wanted me to know what was going on. Their vehicle pulled into the driveway and I was there to open the door and get my hug. She seemed normal, everything was stuffed, and life was fine. I asked her how her week was and received an empty, "Fine." I kept asking questions and they were answered with the same void reply. There was no fear, no regret, no nothing; it was all fine.

So we led her horse out of the pasture and went to work, cleaning the grime out of her horse's winter coat. Not too much was said except light conversation and laughter. I have learned in working with kids that I cannot change them. I am not the Holy Spirit and I cannot draw them to God. I cannot be their Savior, but I can sure point them to their Savior. In 1 Corinthians 13, God says that without love we are nothing. He says that we can speak with the tongues of men and of angels, but if we do not have love, we are nothing more than a clanging gong or a resounding cymbal. There is no point in talking if we do not first show love.

I have tried the first part over the years—speaking truth and wisdom into a situation, thinking that they would see the obvious truth of what God says and instantly change. It has never worked out very well. Working at Sky View, I am learning that the simple act of loving—despite the conditions, the hurts, and the pains—has opened far more doors than ever would have opened had I simply told them what was right and expected them to change.

I looked at my young girl instead of talking through the horrors of suicide, the fear of lying in a bed with a freshly pumped stomach wondering if your liver is going to shut down, and the way God would have her live differently, I chose to simply love her. So we laughed. We told each other funny stories. I asked her about dreams she had for the future and we played. She sat on her horse while we visited.

The world around us was frozen. It had not been above freezing for around a week and the outdoors was an icy wonderland. The creek that runs behind the tack room was frozen in glorious designs; foliage was stiff and cold, awaiting the sappy warmth of spring. The horses' hoofprints that had filled with water were frozen but were remarkable in that they did not freeze solid. They touched the ground in various places, but if you pulled one up, they were shaped in multiple layers and designs.

I pulled a hoofprint sculpture up and showed her the intricate details. Then imagination's glint took over and I started to create a castle out of my ice. There were ridges that became walls, towers that held princesses, and grounds for the soldiers to practice on. She seemed to think I was crazy for a moment and then some walls melted in her heart and she needed a castle. I handed her a lovely frozen hoofprint and through mittened hands, she began to point out the greatness of her castle.

We played at that for a long time—me beside her horse, both of us holding ice and laughing. I have wondered what her mom was thinking as we just stood there talking. Both of our imagined castles became great structures, hers was impenetrable and mine was easily defended.

Then the unthinkable happened and she sent her armies to attack my castle. I fought them off with ease through my heavily guarded walls. She sent another giddy attack. I fended them off and sent one back her way. The battle raged for a few minutes and then the war was over. Neither one of us won and our castles still stood frozen and clear. It was a glorious time of laughter, seeing her imagination come to life and watching a little girl play with something so beautifully simple as frozen water.

At that point I told her I had another thing to show her. She climbed off her horse and followed me with anticipation up the hill. We have a flat place where we plan to put a building someday. With the rain we had had over the winter, many puddles had accumulated. Then the frozen weather hit and I led her out onto our ice skating rink. Another adventure to show her the fullness of life. I instructed her in the fine art of skating in boots and led her out.

We skittered across the puddles, stopped to investigate the beauty of the bubbles frozen in mid-climb through the ice and she giggled. Shrieks of laughter pealed through the frozen air as we slipped and skated around. She became the test pilot for some of the puddles that had not been skated yet. If she did not fall through, then the rest of us might stand a chance—so with a running start she skated across. They held her weight and I followed in one sliding motion.

We simply played; enjoying life and slowly light came back into her eyes. Adventure, love, and laughter had refilled a void. We puffed clouds of frozen breath as we traipsed back down the hill. On our way back to their car we picked up our hoofprint. I watched as a breathless, happy little girl showed her mom all the ins and outs of her castle—the fierceness of its attacking abilities and the beautiful gardens where the princesses play. Her mom watched her little girl. The light of life was in her eye. It was all I could do for her: remind her that there is a reason to live. Life truly is remarkably good if you give it a chance. I had set what I could of God's love before her. Her heart had to respond to His call to the ultimate adventure of life: service to Him.

Twenty-Two

Fingernail Polish

I stood in the shade of the Ponderosa pine right by the edge of the arena watching as small hands with bright pink fingernail polish maneuvered a huge horse around the arena. Concentration flashed on her face, but only through her blinding smile. It was beautiful. I smiled when I remembered that only a few months ago, a timid teenage girl had to be coaxed and convinced out of the car to even pet the horse. I had stepped into her life and challenged her with so many things. Her first ride was spent clinging to the back of Satin, all 86 pounds tight with fear. Riding a horse was a terrifying thing for my sweet girl, but slowly through the first lesson, we worked through the stiff terror.

I began to think over the months and all the hard things I had asked her to do. I became well acquainted with the terrified look that would cross her face the split second before she would hide the fear and do what I asked. First, she learned to ride without a death grip on the saddle, then to stand in the stirrups while the horse walked. Slowly but surely, the movement of the horse became familiar and the saddle became a comfortable place. The horse became a place where she belonged and from which could share her life; the saddle was safe.

As she became familiar with the movement of a horse, she began to talk—never anything deep, just teenage snacks, tripping on the way to the school bus, and the trials of high school cross country, but I knew far more than she let on. Her father was verbally abusive. Days at home were hard; life was not easy in any sense of the word. So she came, week after week, shrieking at the slime of horse saliva while slipping the bit into the horse's mouth, risking chipped nail polish on saddling a horse and spoiling the smell of her perfume with the earthy smell of a warm horse.

Every time she came to the ranch looking like a puppy that had been kicked, I knew there had been trouble at home. We would saddle Satin and laugh. She was unwilling to share what was wrong, but her eyes would flash as she told me stories of things that struck her funny that week. From Satin's back, hours of conversation were had, things that had delighted her during the week were shared and laughter would ripple through the trees; a release of joy.

Then one day she and I were riding together. She'd been willing to risk the weather; we rode beneath dark, looming rain clouds. As we rode, I realized I had mistimed our trail ride. We were a quarter mile from the truck and we were going to get wet. The skies broke and the glory of a storm poured around us. Lightning flashed, followed by thunder and a drenching rain. The torrential rain soaked through in moments. Our horses bowed their necks, trying to keep the rain off their faces. We fought their instincts to turn their backs to the rain in desperate need to get to the truck. I wondered how she would respond. Her hair would be ruined, makeup soaked, and clothes muddy, but then I heard it—laughter. She was laughing in the storm. Giggles of delight ricocheted off raindrops as we raced to cover. Lighting danced and thunder rolled mingled with the glorious sound of joy.

As we threw soaking-wet tack into the truck, I realized again that I could not save her. There was nothing I could do about the hurt and pain at home, but I could offer her a refuge in the midst of the storm, the height of a horse to view life from, laughter, unconditional love, and a place to simply be a girl growing up—despite living in a hard world. She was soaked and smiling bigger than I had seen before.

It was an honor to get to be there as she stepped out of the car into safety each week. One day she was especially excited when she told me, "Hannah, I finally did it! I went to the doctor and I finally weigh over 100 pounds!" She had weighed in at 103 pounds. My little girl was growing up. I paused, looked worried and shook my head, "Well, we're going to have to get you a bigger horse." Concern flashed through her as she looked up at Satin's looming frame. "Really?" I shook my head and she realized she had been teased, laughter rippled. Our lesson had begun; freedom had been given.

Burdens

I'm setting down my burden
I lay it at Your feet
And I'm picking up a new one
It's Yours so light and sweet

You called me to love Your people
To show them Your tender care
You called me to walk with them
But not their burdens bear

For You promised me an easy yoke
A burden You have borne
So that I may walk with You unburdened
Through a world so weighty and torn

So I'll sit and hear of their sorrows
I'll cry with them through the pain
But You'll soon find at the foot of the cross
Each weight and tear has been lain

HANNAH SWAYZE

For You didn't call me to carry
The weight of the world around
So I'll trod through life, my Beloved
With Your burden that I'm glad that I found

— Hannah Swayze

Twenty-Three

Barefoot Summer

As a kid, it truly felt like summer when I was barefoot and riding my horse to the blackberry patch down the dead end road we lived on. We would stroll casually to the wall of berries; if I could not reach the berries from Faith's back I would climb off and start picking. Faith would wait, watching me for her cue. If I picked her a few blackberries then I was stuck. She would stand patiently or sometimes impatiently, waiting for me to pick her allotment of berries. If I did not start off picking her any she would pull her big soft lips back, bare her dirty teeth, and pick her own snack.

She was not nearly as choosy as I was. I would feed her only the hard black ones that were too sour for me. She would eat entire clumps of berries—ripe or not, stems and all. The excursion was complete when we were both purple-tongued and she was drooling blue froth. It was a wonderful way to live. Today, most kids miss blackberry-picking adventures with a horse—but not at Sky View.

I watched my student lead Erik around. Her ride on her horse had been good and I sent them to explore while I worked with her sister. As her sister trotted circles around me, I watched her exploration out of the corner of my eye. She had found a blackberry patch. She reached for a few and tasted. Then lured by the sweet promise, I watched her hunt for more.

A short while later I heard giggling. When I looked up, I saw Erik calmly eating grass while his little rider was laughing, delighted in the moment. She had climbed under the branches of a tree, almost into a blackberry bush, and was eating the berries. Erik had crawled in right behind her and was eating the grass from between the berry vines. Her mouth was beginning to turn blue as Erik grazed around her. They had found the sweetness of summer.

As her sister continued to work around me, I looked up again as the cream of Erik's mane bounced beside the flowing brunette hair of my student running by. She was giggling as he trotted beside her, following her lead like a puppy. A young girl who came to the ranch a few years ago, who had never even led a horse, had the horse she loved trotting beside her as they both enjoyed the sweet essence of life, the gift of a warm summer day.

Twenty-Four

Identity

It was a day almost three years in the making. We both sat on horses in the warmth of the summer sun. I watched pain cross her face and her chin quiver as she described the crumbling walls of her life—her security was falling at her feet. Life as she knew it was a mess. I watched tears flood her eyes, then slowly subside many times over the course of our conversation. My mind worked overtime in an effort to find words that would bring healing–what would help?

As we talked I climbed off my horse and stood at her knee. The mess of all she was going through continued to flow out through broken sentences. Friends abandoning her, those in whom she had found security were walking out of her life, and trust had been broken beyond measure. We were wading into waters I had never explored; I had no experience in the areas she was walking through. I had no idea what to say or do that would help. Then it came, whispered, where He usually gives me the words: Jesus. It was all that came—His name, so sweet and clear, spoken so softly. All I could say, all I would ever have to offer her was Jesus.

So I looked up at her sitting on her horse and extended the only hope I have to offer—salvation—an identity change with Jesus. Sin-stained garments could be swapped for righteousness, the grace and love and peace of Jesus. Instead of backing away from His name, like I assumed she would do because she had in the past, she nodded, listening. So I continued introducing her to the God she had run from for so long. He had been misrepresented to her through flawed people and she had questioned Him, hated Him, and pushed Him away for so long.

Then God took over. My words were not my own, as the Creator of the universe stepped through the broken rubble of her walls to extend a scarred hand into her life.

As she talked, she explained that she had seen people sold out and in love, worshipping God; she was enthralled by the beauty of it. Conversations we had had in the past about Christianity being a relationship, not a religion, came pouring out; she had been listening. Through it all, she had seen it: God's love despite her rejection, His pursuit despite the lack of interest. I listened as her heart poured out all it was feeling. Thought after thought wove itself into the most beautiful picture—a heart pursued in the most passionate way by the love of the King. It was beautiful to see Him alluring her.

I had the honor of offering the proposal of the most passionate love story in the world. I extended the offer of salvation to a girl on a horse as the sun beat down on us. All of creation seemed to hold its breath.

Auburn hair and hazel eyes nodded in agreement, she was ready for salvation. The moment had come.

What followed was the brutally honest, heartfelt prayer of a teenager.

"Hey God, yeah, it's been awhile. . ."

In the simple words that followed, simply asking for forgiveness, her sin-stained garments were taken and she was clothed with the pure righteousness of Christ. The old passed on and she became a new creation. And from the rubble of her identity she emerged a child of God.

When her conversation with God was done, we visited a moment longer and then I asked her, "Who are you?"

A deep, raw, open sparkle flashed through the beauty of her hazel eyes.

"I am a child of God."

Identity was established and all of Heaven rejoiced.

Twenty-Five

The Smile

I would love to say that she effortlessly guided the horse around the arena, but the truth is that while Sabrina was still rather uncomfortable with the idea of being on a horse's back, she was riding a horse who was completely confident with the idea of a rider. I watched and helped where I could, as the horse asked the girl over and over if she was worthy of telling her what to do and testing to see if she was capable.

Talking my unbalanced young student through each little struggle, I prayed she would not get frustrated and give up on riding. But she stuck with it—pulling Satin's head back toward the outside of the circle while keeping her moving. It was a challenge, but her timid little self was up to it so she pressed on. It was the roughest day she would have while riding. In the weeks before, she had been led as she learned balance and then the horse had simply walked as Sabrina worked on keeping Satin moving and asking her to stop. Now I was making her combine everything she had learned and give the horse directions on top of it all.

If she could make it through today, she would be fine.

I watched as concentration furrowed her eyebrows and kept her beautiful smile hidden. Until all at once everything clicked. As everything fell into place, for a brief moment all was right with the world—for she was simply a little girl riding a huge horse.

And she smiled.

As the horse's movement eclipsed the pain of life and an abusive home environment, Sabrina ducked her head and smiled a soft contented smile. She had accomplished something great.

In that moment, I saw not a teen with troubles at home and security issues but rather a beautiful, contented little girl.

Twenty-Six
The Trials in the Trail

Our world was dry at Sky View when I was on a trail ride with one of my beloved students. We had woven through the twists and turns of our trails on the lower, forested half of our property. Janna and I had wound through great Ponderosa pine trees, past cedar trees and eventually headed up our hill. I knew that we were going to come out of the trees at the top and that the view would be glorious. It was late in the summer and rain had not fallen in the Willamette Valley for a long time. Sky View was dry and the ground was covered in a fine layer of powdery dust.

I was on Faith and behind me rode Janna on Sweet Grass. She had been riding her for the few years that she had been involved in the ranch. Despite her life-altering disease, Janna embodied joy. Each time she was able to make it up to the ranch was a reality check for me. She would come every opportunity she could find between surgeries.

Janna has a bone disease that necessitates continual corrective surgeries. The name of it rattles off her tongue faster than I can comprehend the meaning, but it has altered her life. The disease causes her legs to grow at different speeds along with many other problems with her bones. To correct her knees, the doctors go in and place a rod in the growth plate of the leg that is growing so that her other leg can catch up. Her surgeries keep her off her feet—much less horses—for long periods of time.

She is frequently gone from the ranch for long stretches while she recovers from her most recent surgery. Her disease has made her small and she looks far younger than most teens her age.

Behind me, she coughed her way up the dusty, dry driveway. Sweet Grass followed closely in the billowing, dusty footprints of Faith. Comments about how she liked the less dusty trail better reached my ears as we rode. I think it was the first time I had ever heard her complain. I smiled and urged Faith forward. I knew what was at the end of the trail I was leading her on.

She was busy keeping her horse moving behind my horse and occupied with breathing dust when I stopped. Sweet Grass came to rest beside me before Janna even took the time to look. It was a glorious day and the valley spread out below us in a blanket of summer's green. I smiled as her eyes lifted and she breathed out a "Wow." She had no idea it was coming until she stopped and took the time to look.

God reached in and touched the moment with a thought. How often do I do that very thing?

I gripe about where He is leading me, complain about the dust on the trail, and am so busy keeping moving that I do not even realize that we are climbing. The altitude does not register until He stops, I almost bump into Him, and looking at His face, I follow His gaze to the trail we have just walked. The twists and turns, the dust and rocks are all forgotten by the beautiful view. He takes my breath away by gently reminding me that every trail He leads me on is good. Whether I see it or not, He makes the view, the end result, far outweigh the dust and tears of the trail. How faithful He is.

Then I look at the life of my beautiful student—her life is forever altered by this disease that does not make sense. Yet she finds the utmost joy in life. I think she has taught me more than I will ever teach her through a simple comment she made. I asked her one day what the best thing in her life was. She smiled the smile of a horse crazy little girl and breathed out, "Horses!" Then in looking to move the conversation I asked her, "So what is the hardest thing in your life?" She was following me on Sweet Grass as we explored part of the ranch. I was expecting to open up a conversation about the hardships of life and how to get through them.

Instead of complaining about the hardship of living life in and out of hospitals, my little lady so willingly and joyfully lets God lead her ever higher on the trail of life so that one day she can look back at all they have traveled together. I can just hear the awe and wonder of her heart as He reveals to her all that He has done through the trials along the trail of her life. She shocked me with her perspective and I was glad my back was to her. I was glad to hide the smile that crossed my face when, from behind me, I heard her answer my question. It was said with discouraged disgust and I knew exactly how she felt. The hardest thing in her life was not the hospitals, the surgeries, or the effects of the curse; it was simply math.

"Cantering feels like a road trip, it's just kinda bumpy!"

Twenty-Seven

Adventure's Thrill

He stepped onto the ranch, excited to be outside. I extended my hand to his grandmother. They had simply come for a tour of the ranch. His eyes danced, though, as he walked around. I shared our vision with the grandmother and watched him explore. As we talked he was drawn by the electric fence, and I instructed him not to touch it. It made his curiosity pull even harder in the direction of the fence. He was ready to try new things, anything.

We continued talking and I watched as he held a piece of grass on the electric fence. He was not touching it, but he was close. His grandmother reacted and he backed off, but was soon lured back by the unknown. I finally told him to touch it. "You're so curious, you need to just touch it." I knew the shock would satisfy his interest, but when I told him he was allowed to, he could not muster the courage to touch it. He toyed with the idea then walked away. It was too scary.

I finished the tour and ended the day with David as a new student. We had scheduled him to come up and ride on a regular basis. He was struggling with school, his mother had abandoned him at age three, and all he knew from his dad and his dad's girlfriend was to settle disagreements by throwing fists. Needless to say, at eight he was gaining a poor reputation for himself at school.

The following week, I let David meet Stripe—a glorious adventure to challenge his imagination awaited. The first few rides were easy; he grasped the concept of staying on and directing a horse with ease. The only struggle we had was keeping his busy mind occupied long enough to let his body get used to riding. I have many "games" that I teach students to help them use good horsemanship and ride well. He was the inspiration behind all of them. He moved rocks from post to post, laughing as he worked to keep the whole pile of them balanced with him in the English saddle. Then he would ride to a rock on a post, change direction, find another one, and change again.

I had to let him out of the round pen to keep him busy so we rode in the big arena. Nothing fazed him and as we worked, we talked. Stripe was new to the ranch at that point and she was still fighting the herd, looking for her spot in the pecking order. We chatted, him riding Stripe and me keeping pace, about how horses settle their issues by fighting, but that is not how God made us to settle our issues. He started doing better in school.

Summer passed sweetly as I looked forward to the challenge of keeping David's mind busy and his desire for adventure filled. He also won my heart in many ways. One hot day in particular, I was dreading the heat of standing in the arena during his lesson when his grandmother called me. "David was hoping to take you out for lunch instead of riding today." I readily accepted.

Instead of blue jeans and a hat, I dressed up in a cool skirt and met them at the little café. When I walked through the door, I was met by a young boy, grinning from ear to ear, with his usually unruly blond hair combed obediently to the side. We ordered sandwiches and looked at the artwork until they were ready. Lunch was devoured—a mere intrusion in our adventure of exploring the world.

We talked about school and things he was doing over the summer while he ate his sandwich and slurped down his Italian soda. Then, under his grandmother's instruction, he begrudgingly shared his cinnamon roll with me. It was delicious.

The coffee shop had gardens that he wanted to see and to our great delight, we found the little ponds around the courtyard had goldfish. We splashed and wiggled our fingers—trying to lure them out to where we could see them—counted the fish, laughed at their antics, and enjoyed the sunlit flashes of gold with the sheer delight of a child. It was a beautiful time.

The next week I once again had the task of fulfilling the adventure that a ranch should hold for the imagination of a boy. He came and this week it would not be enough to ride a plain brown horse with an English saddle. He wanted a spotted one that he could ride with a Western saddle, a "real" saddle. So we started our day with a horse-hunting adventure through the woods, in search of Satin. She had recently earned her rest after a lesson and had just been set free.

We found her and David sat on her while I led her back to the tack room. Much to her chagrin, she was saddled. A look in her eye told me that she just could not do another lesson in a small pen so I declared it a "blackberry-hunting adventure" day and we set off. A happy cowboy, astride his steed, and the horse—rejoicing in the fact that I was giving her a break by leading her—followed me into the woods.

We found many blackberries—juicy, sweet ones and hard, sour ones. All of them had one little berry segment pulled off and tasted by the blackberry connoisseur on Satin's back. The sweet ones he slurped down and the rejects, after a convincing shudder, we fed to Satin. We ended with his tummy satisfied and another day of desired adventure fulfilled.

In search of keeping my bundle of joyful, all boy happy over the summer, we hunted blackberries, rode Stripe, played rock games, threw a lariat, and found anything else to satisfy. Trotting was another thing to conquer. He handled it with ease. So one hot day, as all summer days are, I challenged him to ride bareback and take on the lesson without a saddle. He enthusiastically accepted, so we brushed and bridled Stripe.

He took the different movement of riding bareback in stride; it was a challenge well worth the excitement. He giggled as she moved and he worked to stay balanced. At the end of the lesson, we stood in the arena. From the molasses-colored back of Stripe, he smiled at me with a flash in his eyes and said, "Now I'm ready to run!"

I laughed and watching him ride, I almost shook my head, thinking about all he had to learn before he was ready to run. There was still balance to master, guiding the horse without so much instruction and time in the saddle before he would be ready. It would be awhile before I let him run.

Later, I thought through it; how often I do that with God. He is leading me on this great adventure, filling the desires I have to see the world, love people, and have and live life to its fullest. He teaches me one thing and I think I have it mastered. Then I tell Him. I'm ready to run.

I did it with Sky View. I had heard stories of ministries like ours—the kids they had impacted and the needs they had met. When we opened our gates, I thought I was so ready to run. There were kids to love, fears to conquer, hurts to heal, and horses to ride. My eyes sparkled with the overwhelming excitement of God reaching through us in exciting moments with children and changing lives.

I thought that every lesson with a kid would lead to huge life changes, tears would wash away hurts, and the love of God would heal instantly when a child encountered a horse. I was ready to run!

God looked at me like I looked at David and shook His head. He loved me and knew that there was no way I was ready to run headlong into the battle of Sky View. So He took my hand, slowed my pace, and began to teach me. We had to learn to crawl through the beginnings of being faithful before we could walk and we must be walking before we learn to run.

David quit coming to the ranch about a year ago and is off on another adventure. He and his dad are doing well, school is going better, and I had the honor of shaking his father's hand as he thanked me for what the Ranch did for his son. Then they turned and walked out of my sphere of influence.

Despite his desire to try new things, David never did touch the fence.

Twenty-Eight
Gracie's Flight

I stepped out of the tack room as I heard their car crunch up the driveway. Delighted freckles met me at the porch. I got the first hug of the day—and with Gracie that is an accomplishment. Normal days, Gracie climbs out of the car and greets the life of the ranch one animal at a time before she comes to me. She pets the horses in the corral, whispering secrets and devout love as she pets noses looking for a treat. Then she checks in with the cows and says hello to Chill the cat. After everyone has been greeted, I am wrapped in the graceful arms of a young girl. Her freckled smile beams through her blonde hair falling out of the ponytail.

Blue eyes dance as she tells me which horse she has planned all week to ride and after donning a helmet, with a halter looped over her shoulder, she skips beside me to the field. Each horse is a beloved friend and is greeted with hugs, kisses, and correction for biting another horse. Life runs on a deeper more passionate level when Gracie is at the ranch.

Gracie entered Sky View several years ago. Her grandparents braved a several hour drive through traffic to get to the ranch for her first lesson. I had met her then, a young girl, fearless, ready to ride anything that smelled, looked, or felt like a horse. The first time she came, her eyes danced with the deep love of a little girl for horses. She had picked our flashiest horse, Sweet Grass and had ridden to her heart's delight. Then distance had caused their family to look for horse lessons closer to their home. An instructor had been found and lessons resumed at a different barn.

What followed was confidence breaking and fear instilling in a little girl. Her instructor worked with her in a large group setting. She was uncomfortable and pushed beyond her comfort zone as she rode while kids barrel raced in the middle of the arena. Then her instructor put her on a new horse that was unfamiliar to her and made her lope. The lesson ended in a puddle of tears from a scared eight-year-old and they never went back.

So I got a call from a mother who had watched her fearless daughter's confidence shatter. Could they come back to Sky View? And the phone call ended with Gracie's name on my calendar.

Her braids and cowgirl boots reflected the love of her life—horses. I got to watch her sparkly eyes dance as she got reacquainted with Sweet Grass. Everything seemed normal: a horse-crazy girl on a girl-crazy horse. I watched and noticed the subtlety of her fear as she chatted and rode. Loping would not be an option for a long time, but with a good horse and a God who heals, it would not take that long to rebuild what had been lost.

After her first lesson, while Gracie unsaddled and began the long process of hugging Sweet Grass goodbye, I got to talk to her mom. Kelli questioned whether her daughter's confidence was restorable and I reassured her that in time Gracie would be fine. With gratitude and lots of hugs, they headed back on the long drive home.

The following week I introduced her to Simon and Erik along with Sweet Grass. I was bringing them down out of the field to be ready for a vet check and as she helped me lead them down, I asked her how she would feel about riding all three of them. Eyes flashed from a freckled face and her braids bounced as she nodded.

Erik was first. His chestnut coat was brushed and she climbed on bareback. I led him and she talked with me. We marveled over the heaviness of his Haflinger step and the roundness of his big back. After informing me that he was probably going to break her pants because he was so wide, we moved to Simon. She liked the tiptoe of his delicate walk and enjoyed the ride immensely. Her mom watched from by the tack room as her daughter had the courage to ride two unfamiliar horses.

When I asked her whom she liked better, Gracie whispered so Simon would not hear, that she liked Erik the best;

then we saddled Sweet Grass. Her ride was good and her confidence even better. As she hugged Sweet Grass and said her
good-byes, I told her mom that she had done really well and
I was glad she was willing to try all three horses. Her list of
whom she wanted to ride had grown. The next week she was
ready to ride Stripe.

An English saddle on a small Arabian mare was quite a
difference from a lumbering Erik, as thudding draft steps were
replaced with the dance of a lighter horse, but she took to
it like a fish to water. By the end of her lesson, I had gotten
to put flesh to something she had read about in one of her
many books. Instead of words on a page, she was feeling the
prancing hoof beats of Stripe's trot. The words she had read
finally made sense as she felt the horse move under her. She
was posting a trot.

Then I let them out of the round pen to adventure on
our little "off road" hills. As she rode, I ducked into the tack
room to grab something, then went to stand by her mom.
Stripe is one of the only horses I have met who can smile with
her whole face and she was smiling as she walked up to Kelli
and me. Behind my back, I had a blue first place ribbon and I
stepped up to Gracie.

At Sky View, we have awards for character qualities that
we see in the kids. Generosity, bravery, and so forth are each
given a number to match the number on the ribbon and
kids can earn different character awards as the staff sees fit. It
started when a horse show group donated a large number of

ribbons. The volunteers and I had racked our brains, thinking through what on earth to do with the two big totes of ribbons we had been given. And as I had watched Gracie, I knew all the options we had talked through were not right. We needed to award character. So I held our first awards ceremony with the smiling Stripe and the beaming Gracie.

I walked up to Stripe's shoulder, and looked up into Gracie's eyes; clear pools of sparkly blue. I told Gracie that for her willingness to get on a horse, and the fact that I had seen her take on her fear of riding with boldness and courage, I had something to give her. I pulled the ribbon out from behind my back: "I would like to award you with our 'Courage' award."

My eyes filled with tears as her jaw dropped. Every horse girl dreams of winning a ribbon and she had just won her blue. She could hardly take her eyes off of it as I hooked her first place ribbon to Stripe's bridle and told her to take her victory lap. Behind me, I could hear Kelli's whisper, "Oh wow!" Gracie turned her little bay around and blond hair and black mane bounced as they took their victory lap.

Gracie's eyes still had not quite seemed to take in all that had just happened, but her mouth had closed by the time they got back. I took the ribbon off her bridle and Gracie climbed off. She stepped back into real life, where horses have to be unsaddled and given treats. As she climbed off, though, I handed her the ribbon and pulled her into a hug. Then reality stood still for just a moment longer as Stripe, always in tune to those around her, wrapped her brown neck and dished face around Gracie and me. Laughing, we both reached out and pulled her horse into our hug as well.

The following week of lessons, Gracie flew. I talked her into a few steps at the canter and my courageous little girl, after only a few weeks of riding, faced her biggest fear. I asked Sweet Grass on the lunge line up into a canter from the middle of the arena as Gracie held a white-knuckled grip on the saddle horn. Her mom wiped tears as she videoed her daughter's success. Fear was conquered and the smile was close to blinding. I received a note in return a few days later.

Dear Hannah,
Thank you for teaching me to fly again.

— Gracie

Resources

Learn more about us on the web at **skyviewhorseranch.org**

Email us with questions at **skyviewhorseranch@gmail.com**

Call our office to schedule a lesson or a tour at
503-829-9800

Read more on Hannah's blog at
http://toviewthesky.blogspot.com/

Get Involved

Schedule to have us come **speak** at your church or organization about Sky View Horse Ranch. **Tell** people you know about our lessons and how to schedule them.

• • • •

Pray for us. We are in a battle against a strong foe, but **He** who is in us is greater!

• • • •

Help sponsor the horses and **fund** the ministry.

Learn about how you can **volunteer** on our website

Acknowledgments

— To my Jesus, You have given me a "Song to sing and a flag to follow." Thank you for the purpose, the kids you have walked into my life, the grace to see each day through at the ranch, and for salvation. Thank you for salvation.

— I would like to thank my family. Daddy, you give me courage to live as a bondservant of Jesus Christ. Mommy, life would not flow without you to talk to. Who else would grab my hand and pray me through life? Rachel, I wanted to be you when I grew up, from wanting as many books as you had on your shelf to finding a family like you had serving Him in Mexico. I found it. Philip, you always have and always will be my hero of a big brother, thank you. Esther, I am so grateful for your friendship; I wish I could communicate God's truths like you do. Abigail, my best friend, you have grown, strengthened, and taught me more than you will ever know. I want to be like you when I grow up. Stephen, you are a man of God and I am so proud, watching your skill with people. I am excited to see what God does with your passion. Samuel, your quiet strength has upheld me so very many times. Be strong and of good courage. Each one of you in my life has made me into the person I am. Thank you for being Swayze.

— A special thanks to anyone who has ever walked, cleared, or built a fence line at Sky View: You are an answer to my prayers.

— To those who have donated time, energy, food, Gatorade, funds, or one of our four-footed staff members: You are amazing. Thank you for placing value on what we do.

— To those who have encouraged me in my writing: Thank you for helping me fulfill this dream.

— Thanks to those who pray for our ministry, the kids, and the staff. You make war on our behalf; thank you.

— A simple thanks to our volunteers seems so small. You are like the men who held up Moses' arms so the Israelites could win the battle. You are the strength we lean on and the encouragement to keep going. I love that several of you have commented that you cannot wait to be old enough to be an instructor. I am so proud of you and the way you represent the ranch. Thank you for being stellar. You win the Hero of the Day award!

— To those at Aloha Publishing, thank you for helping me revive this dream and bring it to completion. You have all been amazing to work with.

— To my friends, whether eating chocolate or hashing life, you know who you are. You could never know how grateful I am for you. God truly is rich in mercy to give you to me. Thanks for wanting to read Beloved, it has meant a lot.

— Staci, thank you for being my sounding board, for praying with me, and sharing heart; I cannot imagine life without you.

— And to my kids: my laughter, and my sunshine. I love you all more than you could comprehend. Why else would I be willing to stand in the hot sun in blue jeans for you?

— And again to my Jesus. Thank you for fulfilling the dreams of my life and for letting me write this book. I love you . . . lots.

About the Author

Hannah Swayze was born into a large, ministry-minded family. From a very young age, she split her time between serving in children's ministry and working with horses. After living in Alaska for a time and working with many children's ministry groups, God called her home for the next phase of her story. In 2012, she and her family began the journey of opening Sky View Horse Ranch. Sky View is a dream come true in her life, as she combines her passion for kids and her love for horses.

Hannah can often be found standing in the arena, talking with a student as they ride around her. She delights in introducing them to the movements of a horse and the love of her King. Many days after the ranch is closed, she spends her time writing and processing the day through pen and paper. The stories she has heard and seen along with the lives she has gotten to meet while working at the ranch were more than she could keep to herself.

In *Beloved,* you will read the stories of a journey: the journey of opening and being director of ministry at Sky View Horse Ranch. The kids she has met and the testimonies of God's redemptive work are woven together in the pages of this book. Hannah shares how dreams are fulfilled and desires met, through being the hands and feet of Jesus to the kids that come up their driveway to ride a horse.

It is her desire to share the incredible joy of walking with the Beloved as He calls us through the adventure of life. Her heart is to see people meet Jesus and be mentored into a deeper love in their walk with God. She is excited to see God doing that through her work on the ranch with the kids and the volunteers that walk through their gates.

Made in the USA
San Bernardino, CA
08 July 2019